MW00352522

BURGOYNE SURROUNDED

A Classic Quilt plus Six Variations

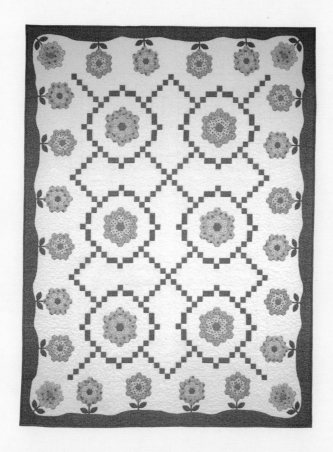

ELIZABETH HAMBY CARLSON

Burgoyne Surrounded:
A Classic Quilt plus Six Variations
© 2004 by Elizabeth Hamby Carlson

That Patchwork Place® is an imprint of
Martingale & Company®.

Martingale & Company
20205 144th Avenue NE
Woodinville, WA 98072-8478 USA
www.martingale-pub.com

No part of this product may be reproduced in any form, unless otherwise stated, in which case reproduction is limited to the use of the purchaser. The written instructions, photographs, designs, projects, and patterns are intended for the personal, noncommercial use of the retail purchaser and are under federal copyright laws; they are not to be reproduced by any electronic, mechanical, or other means, including informational storage or retrieval systems, for commercial use. Permission is granted to photocopy patterns for the personal use of the retail purchaser.

The information in this book is presented in good faith, but no warranty is given nor results guaranteed. Since Martingale & Company has no control over choice of materials or procedures, the company assumes no responsibility for the use of this information.

Printed in China
09 08 07 06 05 04   8 7 6 5 4 3 2 1

Mission Statement

Dedicated to providing quality products and service to inspire creativity.

Acknowledgments

Many thanks to:

Mary Green, Karen Soltys, and all the staff at Martingale for their help and enthusiasm;

Dolores Pilla, for making a beautiful "Fat Quarter Fancy";

Betsy Stein, for volunteering her "Betsy's Burgoyne", and Jean Jarrard for her enthusiasm and valuable second opinions;

Leah Richard and Sheri Flemming for beautiful and timely machine quilting;

My husband, Ken, for his help with all things technical and for his encouragement and support.

Credits

President . . . . Nancy J. Martin
CEO . . . . Daniel J. Martin
Publisher . . . . Jane Hamada
Editorial Director . . . . Mary V. Green
Managing Editor . . . . Tina Cook
Technical Editor . . . . Laurie Baker
Copy Editor . . . . Mary Martin
Design Director . . . . Stan Green
Illustrator . . . . Laurel Strand
Cover Designer . . . . Stan Green
Text Designer . . . . Jennifer LaRock Shontz
Photographer . . . . Brent Kane

Library of Congress Cataloging-in-Publication Data

Carlson, Elizabeth Hamby.
    Burgoyne surrounded : a classic quilt plus six variations / Elizabeth Hamby Carlson.
        p. cm.
Includes bibliographical references.
    ISBN 1-56477-523-2
1. Machine quilting—Patterns. 2. Patchwork—Patterns.
I. Title.
    TT835.C3733 2004
    746.46'041—dc22
                                                            2003027120

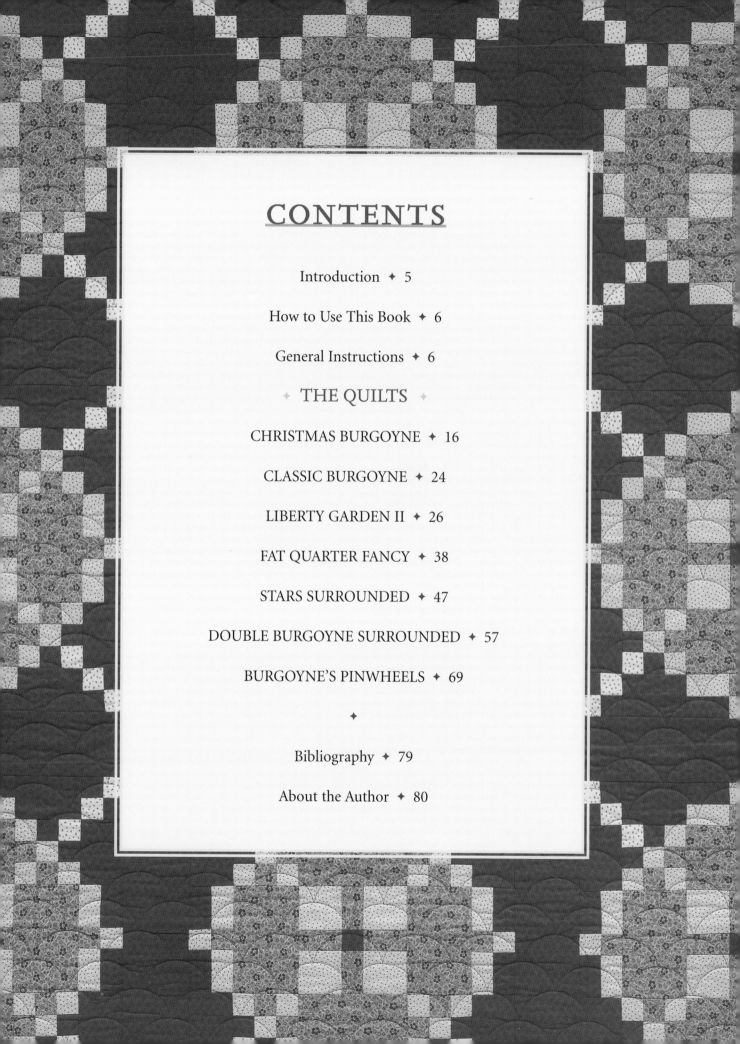

CONTENTS

BURGOYNE SURROUNDED, maker unknown, circa 1890, 76" x 76" (collection of the author).

INTRODUCTION

HISTORY WAS ALWAYS my favorite subject in school, and from early on, I was particularly interested in America's Colonial period. In fifth grade we studied the American Revolution, and I had a small role in a class play about the Battle of Saratoga. At Saratoga, in 1777, a combined force of American militia and Continental regulars surrounded British general "Gentleman Johnny Burgoyne" and seven thousand British troops under his command. Burgoyne, whose forces may have been encumbered by the general's thirty-some carts of personal possessions (including numerous cases of champagne), was forced to surrender to the Americans. The battle proved to be a turning point in America's fight for independence. I played Burgoyne's wife in the play, and though I was playing the wife of a defeated general, I was determined to play it with style.

While on a family trip to Colonial Williamsburg, I had been quite taken with the long, ruffled, and hoop-skirted dresses that the "Colonial ladies" wore. Our class play was my chance to have a Colonial lady dress of my very own! The costume my mother made for me was as authentic as her considerable sewing expertise allowed. And when I wore it I felt like a real eighteenth-century English lady. Because of this small role in a class play, and especially because of my costume, I have always been able to remember the importance of the Battle of Saratoga. My mother saved the costume, and over the years it has been used for dressing up and many more school plays.

Naturally, when I became interested in quilting, the pattern identified as Burgoyne Surrounded caught my attention. The name of this popular pattern is said to reference Burgoyne's defeat at Saratoga. Traditionally done in red and white or in blue and white, the pattern closely resembles a design often found in woven coverlets. In 1932, Stearns and Foster Company, publishers of the Mountain Mist pattern series, copyrighted the pattern and named it "Homespun, Pattern #34."

The pattern's name intrigued me, but I also found myself drawn to the design. The circular pattern has simple but strong graphic appeal, and the diagonal lines connecting the "circles" are reminiscent of an Irish Chain, my favorite pieced pattern. For many years, Burgoyne Surrounded was on the list of quilts I wanted to make. By the time I finally started making it, I also had a number of Burgoyne Surrounded variations on that list of to-be-made quilts.

The block's circular design seemed to me an ideal way to frame pieced or appliquéd designs from other traditional quilt patterns. Once I got started, planning and making these quilts was great fun. Some of the projects, like "Christmas Burgoyne" (page 16), are made entirely of squares and rectangles. Making one of these quilts is a terrific way for beginners to learn rotary-cutting and strip-piecing skills. In "Burgoyne's Pinwheels" (page 69) and the patriotic "Stars Surrounded" (page 47), traditional pieced patterns are framed by the circular piecing. And in "Liberty Garden II" (page 26), the piecing encircles pretty appliquéd hexagon rosettes.

We never know which incidents from our childhood will be remembered and meaningful to us later in our lives. Who would have thought that a class play and a Colonial dress would lead to all these quilts? I hope that you will be inspired to make one or more of these Burgoyne Surrounded quilts and that doing so will create a special memory for you, your family, and your friends.

HOW TO USE THIS BOOK

THE BASIC CONSTRUCTION methods used to make all of the quilts are quite similar. For that reason, tips and techniques for cutting, sewing, and pressing are included in "General Instructions," beginning below. Please take the time to read this section before you get started making the quilts in this book and then refer to the section as needed.

The quilt plan for each project includes yardage, cutting, and sewing information for three different block settings. You may choose a setting of two blocks by three blocks, three blocks by three blocks, or three blocks by four blocks. Additionally, you can choose between two different block sizes for most of the projects. This will enable you to make your quilt the size you would like it to be. The yardage and cutting charts have been color-coded to help you identify the correct information for the quilt size you select.

Please read through all the step-by-step instructions before cutting. The measurements have been checked for accuracy, but always measure your work before cutting borders.

GENERAL INSTRUCTIONS

READ THIS SECTION to become familiar with the techniques and tools used to make the projects, and then refer to it as needed throughout the quiltmaking process.

CHOOSING FABRICS

Most of the quilts in this book use only a few different fabrics, but if you have trouble selecting them, the following information will help you create the look you would like to achieve.

Fabrics for strip-pieced quilts need to be chosen carefully. Strip-piecing means that different areas of the fabric's design will appear at random in the finished quilt. Try to imagine what the fabric you are considering will look like when it is chopped up and put back together randomly. Fabrics with printed motifs that appear to "go every which way" are easier to use than fabrics with strong one-way or linear patterns. One-way or striped fabrics are a problem in the basic

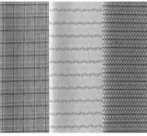

The fabrics in the group on the left do not have a directional pattern and are better suited to strip piecing than those on the right.

Burgoyne Surrounded block because block units need to be rotated within the block to make the design.

Pattern scale and density also are important considerations. Large, widely spaced motifs may look spotty when strip pieced. The relatively small size of the pieces in the Burgoyne Surrounded pattern suggests using medium- to small-scale prints rather than large prints.

WINDOW TEMPLATES: To help see how a fabric will look in your quilt, try viewing it "through the window." Make a window template by cutting a square hole in the middle of an index card or piece of paper. The hole should be the size of the finished squares in your quilt. When you view the fabric through the template, you will be better able to evaluate how a small piece of that fabric will look in your quilt.

BACKGROUND FABRICS: High-value contrast between the background and other fabrics is important to define the pattern. You may choose to use a light background with dark fabric to make the pattern or a dark background with light fabric, as in "Christmas Burgoyne" (page 16).

Neutral fabrics are an easy and traditional choice for the background of your quilt. You can use a single background fabric or many different ones, as in "Fat Quarter Fancy" (page 38).

Suitable Background Fabrics

One easy way to begin the fabric selection is by choosing a multicolored "theme" fabric in colors you like. The theme fabric might be used for borders, as in "Burgoyne's Pinwheels," or for all or part of the background, as in "Christmas Burgoyne." In each case, the fabrics in the quilts were selected because they harmonized with the theme fabric.

I began the fabric selection for "Christmas Burgoyne" (left) and "Burgoyne's Pinwheels" (right) by choosing the theme fabric, shown at the top of each stack. I then chose the remaining fabrics because they coordinated with the theme fabric.

Tools

Making these quilts does not require a lot of fancy equipment, but using high-quality tools that are in good working order will ensure that your sewing time is more pleasant and successful.

Rotary cutter and mat: Choose a cutter that feels comfortable in your hand. The blade should be very sharp. Using a dull blade can result in the layers shifting while cutting. For big cutting jobs, I prefer the extra-large-size Olfa cutter. A rotary mat with grid lines helps you keep the fabric square while cutting. Never use the grid lines for measuring. Always measure with your ruler.

Rotary rulers: You will need a rotary ruler with both vertical and horizontal measuring lines. I find a 6" x 24" ruler is best when cutting long strips. Another smaller ruler is useful for squaring up the fabric.

Sewing machine: Your sewing machine should be in good working order and stitch a straight stitch with even tension.

Quilter's quarter-inch presser foot: If a special quarter-inch foot for quilters is available for your machine, use it to help keep your seam allowances accurate.

Seam ripper, stiletto, or small screwdriver: Use one of these tools to help guide the pieced segments under the presser foot. The tip of these tools can go where your fingers cannot, and should not! Use them to ease fabric and adjust seam allowances that want to flip the wrong way.

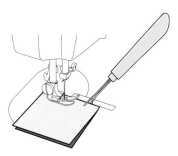

Machine needles: Put a fresh needle into your machine when you start your quilt. Use size 70/10 or 75/11.

Thread: For machine piecing, I use neutral-colored 100%-cotton sewing thread. Light to medium gray seems to blend well with most fabrics. If your fabrics are very dark, use darker thread.

Pins: Straight pins are needed for piecing. I prefer to use very fine silk pins with colored heads.

CUTTING STRAIGHT STRIPS

Follow these steps for perfect, straight strips every time. Instructions are for cutting right-handed; reverse the directions if you are left-handed.

1. Fold and press the fabric in half so the selvages meet. Smooth the fabric so it has no wrinkles, pulls, or puckers.

2. Place the folded fabric on the cutting board with the fold closest to you. Align the bottom edge of a small rotary ruler or quilter's square with the folded edge of the fabric. Place another ruler alongside the left edge of the first ruler.

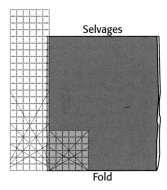

3. Remove the first (smaller) ruler and use your rotary cutter to straighten the fabric's left edge.

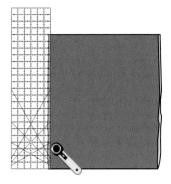

4. Fold up the folded edge so it meets the selvage edges. Use a rotary ruler to make certain the two folded edges are exactly parallel to each other. This is very important: for the strips to be straight, the folds must be parallel, and the newly trimmed edge must be perpendicular to both folds.

5. Repeat steps 2 and 3 to retrim the fabric edge. You are now cutting four layers at once.

6. Align the newly cut edge of the fabric with the ruler markings for the desired strip width. Cut a strip. Then open it to check that it is straight. Continue cutting strips as needed, checking periodically to be sure strips are still straight. If not, repeat the steps for folding and aligning fabric.

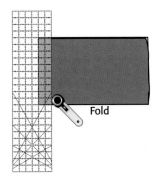

Fold

SEWING ACCURATE SEAMS

The success of your quilt depends on sewing accurate and consistent ¼"-wide seams. In my classes I help students set up their machines with a seam guide, even those students who are sure they don't need one. Inevitably, they are amazed at the improvement in their accuracy. Make a seam guide for your machine and sew a set of test strips following these steps:

1. Place either ¼" graph paper or the ¼" mark on a rotary ruler directly under the needle on your machine. Be sure the ruler or paper excess extends to the left of the needle. Lower the needle until it pierces either the ¼" marking on the graph paper or just touches the marking on the ruler. Make sure the ruler or paper is straight by aligning a horizontal line on the machine with a horizontal line on the ruler or graph paper. (The edge of the throat plate makes a good guide.) Then lower the presser foot to hold it in place.

2. Right along the edge of the ruler or paper, just in front of the feed dogs and exactly ¼" to the right of the needle, stack several pieces of 1"-long

masking tape. Align the long edges of the tape that are closest to the needle. As an alternative, you can use adhesive-backed moleskin, which is sold for foot care. It is sold in two thicknesses; I use the thinner of the two and cut a ½" x 1" piece. It provides a slightly thick, straight edge and eliminates the need to layer. Cut a moleskin seam guide with a rotary cutter (using an old blade) to ensure a clean straight edge.

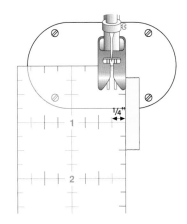

3. Check the accuracy of your seam guide by cutting three 1½" x 6" test strips: two dark and one light. Sew a dark strip to the light strip. Press the seam toward the dark strip, and then measure the distance from one raw edge to the seam line: it should measure exactly ¼".

4. Sew the remaining dark strip to the remaining long raw edge of the light strip in the previously sewn pair. Press the new seam toward the dark strip. If the seam allowances are accurate, the center strip will measure 1". If not, try again!

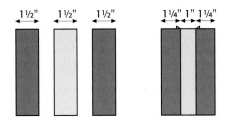

MAKING STRIP SETS

Most of the units in these quilts are made with strip-piecing techniques. Strips are first sewn together into strip sets. Then the strip sets are crosscut and sewn into units. Sewn and pressed strip sets should be even, flat, and straight. Follow these tips for perfectly accurate strip sets.

1. Place two adjacent strips right sides together, aligning the top and the long raw edges, and pinning if necessary. Sew the strips together from top to bottom, stopping periodically (with the needle down) to realign the raw edges as needed. Do not pull on the strips as you sew; allow the machine's feed dogs to move the fabric along.

2. Place the sewn pair of strips on the ironing board, with the strip that the seam will be pressed toward on top, and with the seam allowance away from you. "Set the seam" first by pressing it flat. This step helps eliminate any puckers after sewing.

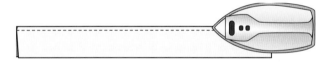

TIP: Set your iron to the cotton setting. I use steam for a good, firm press. Carefully follow the pressing arrows provided with each project so that seam allowances will oppose, or nest, when blocks and rows are sewn together.

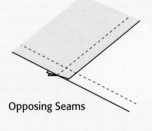

Opposing Seams

3. Open the strips with your fingers and, from the right side of the fabric, press the seam allowance toward the top strip, taking care to fully open and flatten the seam. Be sure to keep the strips straight on the ironing board as you press.

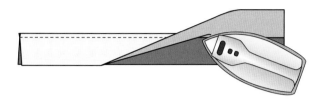

TIP: Always press each seam before sewing another strip to the set. Never sew a strip to an unpressed set!

CROSSCUTTING STRIP SETS

After making the strip sets, the next step is to crosscut them into segments. The segments will be sewn together later to make units. You may crosscut strip sets one at a time or layer them and cut two at once.

Crosscutting Strip Sets Singly

1. Place a strip set horizontally on the cutting board, wrong side up. Align the horizontal lines on a rotary ruler so they are parallel to the seam lines on the sewn strip set. Refer to "Cutting Straight Strips," steps 2 and 3 on page 8, and trim the left edge of the strip set.

2. Align the newly cut edge of the strip set with the ruler markings for the desired segment width.

Double-check that the horizontal lines on the ruler are still parallel to the seam lines of the strip set. Crosscut the desired number of segments.

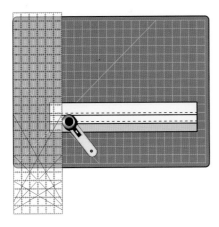

Crosscutting Strip Sets in Layers

Layering and cutting paired strip sets is a real time-saver, and a good way to check for accuracy. Try it once you feel confident with your cutting skills.

When cut segments from two different strip sets are going to be sewn together into units, it is handy to crosscut the strip sets in pairs. Cut this way, the segments are already matched and ready to sew together! For example, most blocks in these quilts have a unit 3 that is a simple nine-patch. In these units, rows 1 and 2 will always be sewn together, so a strip set for row 1 and a strip set for row 2 can be paired together and crosscut into segments. Pairs of cut segments are ready to pick up and sew together; their long edges are already aligned for stitching. Like pairs can be quickly chain-pieced, saving a great deal of time.

When you study the block diagrams for each project, look to identify these "paired segments" in each unit.

To layer and cut pairs of strip sets:

1. Place strip set 1 on the mat, right side up.

2. Place strip set 2 on top of strip set 1, right sides together. If the strip sets have been sewn and pressed correctly, the seam allowances of the sets should nest together perfectly.

3. Follow the steps for "Crosscutting Strip Sets Singly" to straighten the edges and to crosscut the strip-set pair into segments. Do not separate the pairs of segments; they are ready to sew together.

> **TIP:** Use the side of your ruler to gently move the cut pairs of segments. I cut on the large mat on my cutting table. Then I use the ruler to transfer the pairs to a small mat I can carry to my machine. The less the pairs are handled, the better the edges will stay aligned for sewing.

SEWING THE BLOCKS

The blocks are assembled by sewing the cut segments into units and then sewing the units together into blocks.

It is usually not necessary to pin the segments and units for sewing; the nested seam allowances help keep things in place. Use a stiletto or small screwdriver to guide the segments under the presser foot and to adjust or ease as needed. Sew the segments together from seam to seam, pausing (with the needle down) after crossing each seam to assure the next seam is aligned properly. Of course, if pinning makes you feel more secure, then go ahead.

Press each unit before sewing units together into block rows. Following pressing arrows carefully will ensure that the blocks go together smoothly.

ADDING BORDERS

Choosing borders for a quilt is much like choosing a frame for a picture. Whenever possible, I like to wait until the center of the quilt is complete before making a final decision on borders. Generally I have something in mind, but experience has taught me the importance of being flexible. Sometimes the fabric I plan to use for the border does nothing to enhance and frame the quilt, so I have to think again. Admittedly, this can mean buying more fabric, but it is always worth it in the end. Before you cut your borders, audition the fabric, or combination of fabrics, to find a choice just right for your quilt.

Border measurements are given for projects that include borders, but because variations in size can occur during quilt construction, always measure your own work before cutting borders.

Straight-Cut Borders

Straight-cut borders are the simplest to make. The side borders are the same length as the body of the quilt and are added first. The top and bottom borders are the width of the quilt body plus the width of the two side borders. When a quilt has inner and outer straight-cut borders, add the inner border first, and then add the outer border.

1. Measure the length of the quilt top through its center. Cut side borders of the required width to match this measurement. Use a pin to mark the center of each border strip and the center of each side of the quilt. With right sides together, pin the borders to the quilt top, matching the center points and outer edges; stitch. Press the seam allowances toward the borders.

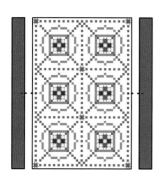 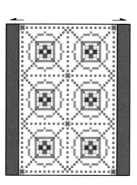

2. Measure the width of the quilt (including the side borders) through its center. Cut the top and bottom borders of the required width to match this measurement. Pin and sew the top and bottom borders to the quilt top as described in step 1. Press the seam allowances toward the borders.

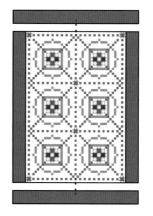 

Mitered Borders

Mitered borders require a little more time and attention than straight-cut borders, but they aren't difficult, and they give a quilt a polished look. They are especially effective when striped fabrics are used (see "Fat Quarter Fancy" on page 44). Cut miter strips the full length or width of the quilt—including borders—plus an extra inch. When the quilt has more than one border to be mitered, cut all the border strips for each side the same length as the outermost border and sew the strips together to create a single border unit.

There are a number of ways to make mitered borders. Because I also like to appliqué, I sew the miters closed by hand. It's a simple method, and because I work from the right side, it's nearly foolproof, especially for multiple or striped borders.

1. Measure the quilt as for straight-cut borders. Estimate the final outside measurements of the

quilt, including the borders, and add 1". Cut the border strips to this length.

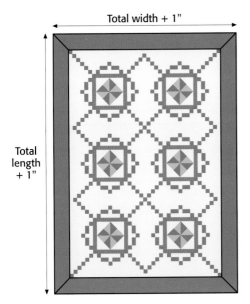

2. Use a pin to mark the center of each border strip and the center of each side of the quilt top. On each border strip, also measure and mark one-half the length (or width) of the quilt top from each side of the center pin.

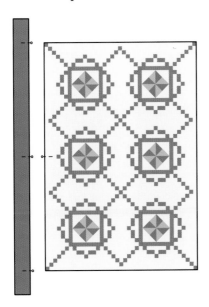

3. Place a border strip and the quilt top right sides together, matching the center points. Also match the outer pins to the raw edges of the quilt top. Sew the border strip to the quilt, beginning and

ending with a backstitch ¼" from the corners of the quilt top. Press the seams toward the border. Repeat on each side of the quilt.

4. To make the miters, lay the quilt on an ironing board so the top border extends over the side borders. Fold under one corner of the top border at a 45° angle, using the 45° marking on your ruler as a guide. Press the fold and pin it securely by placing pins perpendicular to the fold.

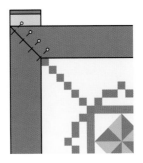

5. Working from the right side, carefully hand sew the mitered corner closed with tiny, invisible hand stitches. Repeat this process for the remaining three corners. Trim the seams to ¼" and press them open.

BACKING AND BATTING

Choose backing fabric that complements the front of the quilt and the binding. The backing should measure approximately 4" larger than the top on all sides. If necessary, seam the backing by dividing it crosswise (selvage to selvage), removing the selvages, and then sewing it down the middle or in three sections. Press the seams open.

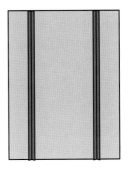

Your choice of batting may depend on your quilting plan. For machine-quilting, I prefer to use a lightweight to medium-weight cotton batting. The quilt will shrink up just a bit when it is washed and help hide the machine stitching, giving the quilt an older look. For hand quilting, I like to use polyester batting because it is much easier for me to needle. Whichever fiber you choose, use a good-quality batting. Many lovely quilts have been ruined by "bargain batting." Too much time and love go into making the top to compromise on what's inside. Cut the batting approximately 3" larger than the top on all sides.

Layering and Basting

Place the backing wrong side up on a clean, flat surface. Center and smooth the batting, and then the quilt top, right side up, over the backing. Baste through all the layers, beginning in the center and working out in each direction; smooth the layers as you go. For hand quilting, baste a 4" grid pattern and finish with a line of stitching all around the outside edge. For machine quilting, baste and secure the layers with safety pins.

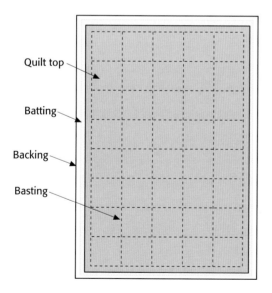

Quilt top

Batting

Backing

Basting

Quilting

The quilting designs you choose will depend on your own preferences and on how you plan to use the quilt. Most of the quilts in this book were machine quilted by a professional using a long-arm quilting machine. They were made for use on beds and may have hard wear, so professional machine quilting was a durable and time-efficient choice.

For machine quilting, straight lines or continuous-line patterns are neat and easy. Use an even-feed, or walking, foot on your machine so the layers will move through the feed dogs evenly. Set your machine at 8 to 10 stitches per inch, and remove the safety pins as you sew.

Hand quilting is a lovely way to finish a quilt and is especially nice on a traditional quilt with a plain background and sashing to show off your stitching. My antique Burgoyne Surrounded (page 4) was beautifully quilted with straight feather plumes in the sashing strips, single-line cross-hatching in the blocks, and paired diagonal lines in the borders. Most quilters prefer to hand quilt in a hoop or a frame. Begin quilting in the center of the quilt and work out in each direction to avoid puckers and bumps.

If you wish to use an elaborate quilting pattern in the borders or sashing strips, such as feathers or cables, mark the top before it is layered and basted. If your quilting plan is simple, like outline or straight-line quilting, you can mark as you go. Always test your marking tool to be sure the marks can be removed.

Binding

Instructions for all projects in this book include yardage required for bias binding. Bias binding is a good choice for quilts likely to be well used.

1. Use a rotary cutter to trim the backing and batting even with the edges of the quilt top, and to square the quilt corners. Baste the three layers together

around the edge to prevent shifting as you apply the binding.

2. Total the outside dimensions of the quilt (the perimeter) and add 9". Cut enough 2½"-wide bias strips from the binding fabric to equal this measurement. Join the strips with diagonal seams. Trim the seam allowances to ¼" and press them open.

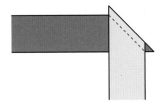

3. Trim one end of the long strip at a 45° angle, and turn under a ¼" hem. Press the binding in half lengthwise, wrong sides together.

Fold line

4. Lay the binding on the front of the quilt, aligning all raw edges. Place the end of the binding approximately 10" from a corner. Begin stitching 4" from the end of the binding, taking a ⅜" seam allowance. Stop stitching ⅜" from the first corner and backstitch.

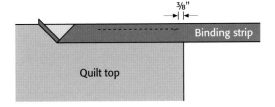

⅜"

Binding strip

Quilt top

TIP: Use a heavier machine needle to sew the binding to the quilt. I use a 90/14. To keep the layers from shifting while you stitch, use a walking foot when applying the binding. This special presser foot, also used for machine quilting, allows multiple layers to feed through the machine at the same rate.

5. Fold up the binding so that it creates a 45° angle and is perpendicular to the edge you just stitched. Refold the binding straight down so the corner fold is even with the edge of the quilt. Start sewing at the folded edge, beginning with a backstitch, and continue stitching around the remaining edges and corners until you are 4" from the starting point.

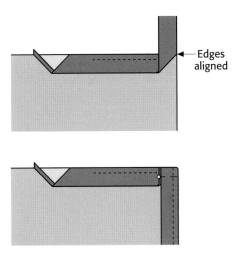

Edges aligned

6. Trim the end of the binding so it overlaps the beginning by 3". Tuck the cut end of the binding strip inside the diagonal fold. Be sure that the join is smooth on the long folded edge. Pin and finish sewing the binding to the quilt.

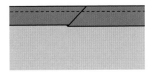

7. Fold the binding over the edge of the quilt and hand stitch it to the backing with an invisible hand stitch. As you fold each corner back, a miter will form on the front. To make a similar miter on the back, fold down one side of the binding and then the other. Finish the binding by hand, stitching the diagonal folds of the miters and the diagonal seam where the binding ends.

CHRISTMAS BURGOYNE

A rich red background and a pretty green floral print give this classic quilt a festive air, but don't be afraid to display it year-round. Refer to the "Finished Quilt Sizes" chart on page 17 to see what options are available, and then follow the block size and quilt plan for your selected quilt size throughout the instructions.

FINISHED BLOCK SIZES (Choose one.)

Block	Block Size
A	15"
B	18¾"

FINISHED QUILT SIZES

Block	2 x 3 Blocks	3 x 3 Blocks	3 x 4 Blocks
A	39" x 57"	57" x 57"	57" x 75"
B	48¾" x 71¼"	71¼" x 71¼"	71¼" x 93¾"

MATERIALS: 42"-WIDE FABRIC

Block A

Fabric	2 x 3 Blocks	3 x 3 Blocks	3 x 4 Blocks
Red (block backgrounds)	2⅛ yards	2⅞ yards	3½ yards
Green (block backgrounds)	⅞ yard	1¼ yards	1⅜ yards
White print (blocks)	1 yard	1⅝ yards	1⅝ yards
Backing	3½ yards	3½ yards	4½ yards
Binding	⅞ yard	⅞ yard	1 yard
Batting	45" x 63"	63" x 63"	63" x 81"

Block B

Fabric	2 x 3 Blocks	3 x 3 Blocks	3 x 4 Blocks
Red (block backgrounds)	3 yards	3⅝ yards	4¾ yards
Green (block backgrounds)	1¼ yards	1¾ yards	2⅛ yards
White print (blocks)	1⅝ yards	1⅞ yards	2½ yards
Backing	4¼ yards	4¼ yards	5⅝ yards
Binding	⅞ yard	1 yard	1 yard
Batting	55" x 77"	77" x 77"	77" x 100"

CUTTING STRIPS

Cut the required number of strips in the appropriate width to make the quilt size you have chosen. Cut all strips across the full width of the fabric, selvage to selvage. All measurements include ¼"-wide seam allowances. Refer to "Cutting Straight Strips" (page 8) for additional guidance as needed.

NUMBER AND WIDTH OF STRIPS

Block A

Fabric	Cut Width	2 x 3 Blocks	3 x 3 Blocks	3 x 4 Blocks
Red	1½"	11	15	16
	2½"	7	11	13
	3½"	9	12	16
Green	1½"	4	8	8
	2½"	2	2	2
	3½"	4	6	7
White	1½"	12	19	20
	2½"	4	8	8

Block B

Fabric	Cut Width	2 x 3 Blocks	3 x 3 Blocks	3 x 4 Blocks
Red	1¾"	15	16	19
	3"	10	12	17
	4¼"	9	12	16
Green	1¾"	7	8	11
	3"	2	2	2
	4¼"	5	8	10
White	1¾"	19	20	27
	3"	6	8	10

CHRISTMAS BURGOYNE

By Elizabeth Hamby Carlson, 2003, Montgomery Village, Maryland, 71" x 71". Quilted by Leah Richard.

MAKING THE BLOCK UNITS

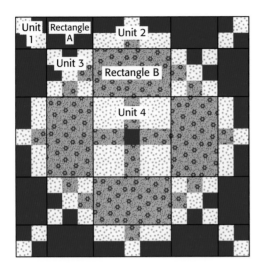

The Burgoyne Surrounded block is made up of four units and two different sizes of background rectangles. The units and rectangles are the same in each block. Follow the step-by-step instructions to make each unit, referring to the chart to find the number of units required for the size quilt you have chosen. Note that the number of units and rectangles required is the same for both block sizes. The cutting instructions for the background rectangles will be given later.

UNIT REQUIREMENTS

Unit	2 x 3 Blocks	3 x 3 Blocks	3 x 4 Blocks
One	24	36	48
Two	24	36	48
Three	24	36	48
Four	6	9	12

Unit 1

1. Make the required number of strip sets for the quilt size you have chosen, using one red and one white strip per set. For block A quilts, use 1½"-wide strips. For block B quilts, use 1¾"-wide strips. Refer to "Making Strip Sets" (page 10) as needed.

NUMBER OF STRIP SETS

Block	2 x 3 Blocks	3 x 3 Blocks	3 x 4 Blocks
A	2	3	4
B	3	4	5

2. Crosscut the strip sets into segments the same width as the strip width used to make the strip sets (1½" or 1¾"). Refer to "Crosscutting Strip Sets" (page 8) for guidance. Note that the number of segments to cut is the same for both block sizes.

NUMBER OF SEGMENTS

2 x 3 Blocks	3 x 3 Blocks	3 x 4 Blocks
48	72	96

3. Stitch two segments together as shown to make unit 1.

Unit 1

Unit 2

1. Make strip sets for rows 1 and 2 as shown, using two red or white wide strips and one white or green narrow strip per set. For block A quilts use 1½"- and 2½"-wide strips. For block B quilts use 1¾"- and 3"-wide strips. Note that the number of strip sets to make is the same for each row.

Row 1

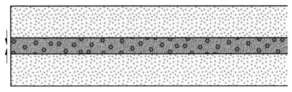

Row 2

NUMBER OF STRIP SETS
(Make this number for each row.)

Block	2 x 3 Blocks	3 x 3 Blocks	3 x 4 Blocks
A	1	2	2
B	2	2	3

2. Crosscut the strip sets into segments the same width as the narrow strip width used to make the strip sets (1½" or 1¾"). Cut one segment from both the row 1 and row 2 strip sets for each unit 2 required.

3. Sew one row 1 segment and one row 2 segment together as shown to make unit 2.

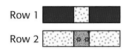

Unit 2

Unit 3

1. Make strip sets for rows 1, 2, and 3 as shown, using the red, white, and green strips. For block A quilts, use 1½"-wide strips. For block B quilts, use 1¾"-wide strips. Note that the number of strip sets to make is the same for each row.

Row 1

Row 2

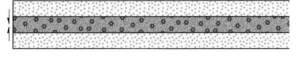

Row 3

NUMBER OF STRIP SETS
(Make this number for each row.)

Block	2 x 3 Blocks	3 x 3 Blocks	3 x 4 Blocks
A	1	2	2
B	2	2	3

2. Crosscut the strip sets into segments the same width as the strip width used to make the strip sets (1½" or 1¾"). Cut one segment from the row 1, 2, and 3 strip sets for each unit 3 required.

3. Sew one each of the row 1, 2, and 3 segments together as shown to make unit 3.

Unit 3

Unit 4

1. Make strip sets for rows 1 and 2 as shown, using two white or green wide strips and one green or red narrow strip. For block A quilts use 1½"- and 2½"-wide strips. For block B quilts use 1¾"- and 3"-wide strips.

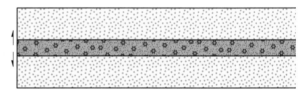

Row 1

Row 2

NUMBER OF STRIP SETS

Block	Row	2 x 3 Blocks	3 x 3 Blocks	3 x 4 Blocks
A	1	1	2	2
	2	1	1	1
B	1	1	2	2
	2	1	1	1

2. Crosscut the strip sets into the required number of segments. Cut row 1 segments 2½" wide (block A) or 3" wide (block B). Cut row 2 segments to the same width as the narrow width used to make the strip sets (1½" or 1¾"). Note that the number of segments to cut is the same for both block sizes.

NUMBER OF SEGMENTS

Row	2 x 3 Blocks	3 x 3 Blocks	3 x 4 Blocks
1	12	18	24
2	6	9	12

3. Sew two row 1 segments and one row 2 segment together as shown to make unit 4.

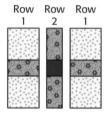 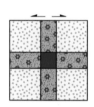

Row 1 Row 2 Row 1

Unit 4

CUTTING THE BACKGROUND RECTANGLES

Crosscut the red 2½"-wide strips (block A) or 3"-wide strips (block B) into background rectangle A. For block A quilts, cut the rectangles 2½" x 3½". For block B quilts, cut the rectangles 3" x 4¼". Crosscut the green 3½"-wide strips (block A) or 4¼"-wide strips (block B) into background rectangle B. For block A quilts, cut the rectangles 3½" x 5½". For block B quilts, cut the rectangles 4¼" x 6¾". Note that the number to cut is the same for both block sizes.

RECTANGLE CUTTING

Rectangle	2 x 3 Blocks	3 x 3 Blocks	3 x 4 Blocks
A	48	72	96
B	24	36	48

ASSEMBLING THE BLOCKS

Arrange the units and rectangles into rows as shown. Stitch the units and rectangles in each row together. Press the seams in the directions indicated. Sew the rows together. Press the seams in the directions indicated.

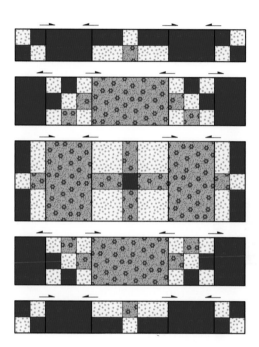

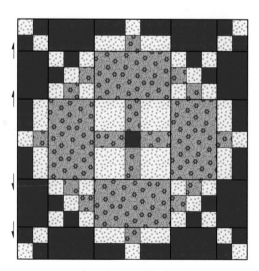

Make 6 for 2 x 3 block quilt.
Make 9 for 3 x 3 block quilt.
Make 12 for 3 x 4 block quilt.

MAKING THE SASHING

1. Crosscut the required number of strips from the red 3½"-wide (block A) or 4¼"-wide (block B) strips. For block A quilts, cut 3½" x 15½" strips. For block B quilts, cut 4¼" x 19¼" strips. Note that the number of sashing strips is the same for both block sizes.

NUMBER OF SASHING STRIPS

2 x 3 Blocks	3 x 3 Blocks	3 x 4 Blocks
17	24	31

2. Make one strip set *each* for rows 1, 2, and 3 of the center, side, and corner sashing blocks as shown, using the red and white strips. For block A quilts, use 1½"-wide strips. For block B quilts, use 1¾"-wide strips.

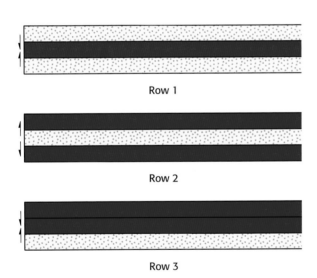

Row 1

Row 2

Row 3

3. Crosscut the strip sets into segments the same width as the strip width used to make the strip sets (1½" or 1¾"). Note that the number of segments to cut is the same for both block sizes.

NUMBER OF SEGMENTS

Row Number	2 x 3 Blocks	3 x 3 Blocks	3 x 4 Blocks
1	10	16	22
2	12	16	20
3	4	4	4

4. Crosscut the red 1½"-wide strips (block A) or 1¾"-wide strips (block B) into rectangles for the side and corner sashing blocks. For block A quilts, cut 1½" x 3½" rectangles. For block B quilts, cut 1¾" x 4¼" rectangles. Note that the number to cut is the same for both block sizes.

ROW 4 RECTANGLES

2 x 3 Blocks	3 x 3 Blocks	3 x 4 Blocks
10	12	14

5. For each block, arrange the segments and rectangles into rows as shown. Stitch the rows together.

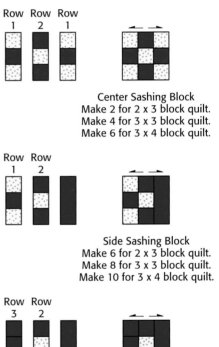

Row 1 Row 2 Row 1

Center Sashing Block
Make 2 for 2 x 3 block quilt.
Make 4 for 3 x 3 block quilt.
Make 6 for 3 x 4 block quilt.

Row 1 Row 2

Side Sashing Block
Make 6 for 2 x 3 block quilt.
Make 8 for 3 x 3 block quilt.
Make 10 for 3 x 4 block quilt.

Row 3 Row 2

Corner Sashing Block
Make 4 for all quilt sizes.

ASSEMBLING THE QUILT TOP

Refer to the quilt diagram to arrange the Burgoyne Surrounded blocks, the sashing rectangles, and the sashing blocks into horizontal rows. The placement of the sashing blocks for the 2 x 3 and 3 x 3 quilt plans will need to be changed slightly from the diagram shown so that the corner sashing blocks are in each corner and the side sashing blocks are positioned along the outside edges of the quilt top with the red rectangle toward the outside of the quilt. Stitch the pieces in each row together and press the seams toward the sashing rectangles. Carefully pin the rows together to match seams. Sew the rows together. Press the seams toward the sashing rows.

FINISHING

Refer to "Backing and Batting" (page 13), "Layering and Basting" (page 14), "Quilting" (page 14), and "Binding" (page 14) as needed.

1. Piece the quilt backing as necessary. Center the quilt top and batting over the backing; baste.

2. Quilt as desired.

3. Trim the backing and batting. Cut the binding fabric into 2½"-wide bias strips. Sew the binding to the quilt.

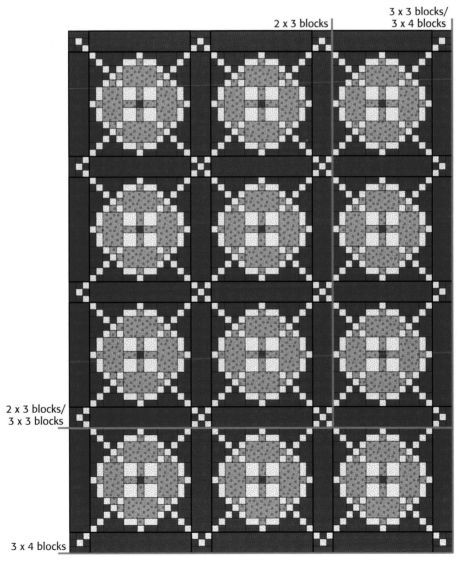

2 x 3 blocks

3 x 3 blocks/
3 x 4 blocks

2 x 3 blocks/
3 x 3 blocks

3 x 4 blocks

Quilt Diagram

CLASSIC BURGOYNE

"Betsy's Burgoyne" by Elizabeth Leahy Stein, 2003, Edgeworth, Pennsylvania,
57" x 75". Quilted by Sheri Flemming.

A book on Burgoyne Surrounded quilts wouldn't be complete without instructions for a two-color quilt, the most traditional version of these quilts. My dear friend Betsy Stein made this one, and it is a perfect example of this well-loved pattern. "Betsy's Burgoyne" is made exactly like my "Christmas Burgoyne" on page 16. If you would like to make Betsy's two-fabric version, follow the "Christmas Burgoyne" instructions, making the following changes to the fabric requirements and cutting instructions.

MATERIALS: 42"-WIDE FABRIC

Block A

Fabric	2 x 3 Blocks	3 x 3 Blocks	3 x 4 Blocks
White (block backgrounds)	2⅞ yards	4 yards	4¾ yards
Red (blocks, binding)	1⅞ yards	2½ yards	2⅝ yards
Backing	3½ yards	3½ yards	4½ yards
Batting	45" x 63"	63" x 63"	63" x 81"

Block B

Fabric	2 x 3 Blocks	3 x 3 Blocks	3 x 4 Blocks
White (block backgrounds)	4¼ yards	5½ yards	7 yards
Red (blocks, binding)	2⅝ yards	3 yards	3⅝ yards
Backing	4¼ yards	4¼ yards	5⅝ yards
Batting	55" x 77"	77" x 77"	77" x 100"

NUMBER AND WIDTH OF STRIPS

Block A

Fabric	Cut Width	2 x 3 Blocks	3 x 3 Blocks	3 x 4 Blocks
White	1½"	15	23	24
	2½"	9	13	15
	3½"	13	18	23
Red	1½"	12	19	20
	2½"	4	8	8

Block B

Fabric	Cut Width	2 x 3 Blocks	3 x 3 Blocks	3 x 4 Blocks
White	1¾"	22	24	30
	3"	12	14	19
	4¼"	14	20	26
Red	1¾"	19	20	27
	3"	6	8	10

CUTTING STRIPS

Cut the required number of strips in the appropriate width to make the quilt size you have chosen. Cut all strips across the full width of the fabric, selvage to selvage. All measurements include ¼"-wide seam allowances. Refer to "Cutting Straight Strips" (page 8) for additional guidance as needed.

INSTRUCTIONS

Follow the instructions for "Christmas Burgoyne" on pages 16–23 to complete "Betsy's Burgoyne," using white in place of the red and green pieces, and red in place of the white pieces.

LIBERTY GARDEN II

The original "Liberty Garden" (page 27) is a small-scale quilt inspired by the Liberty of London floral fabrics I used in the Grandmother's Flower Garden portion of the Burgoyne Surrounded blocks and around the appliquéd borders. While making the small quilt, I kept thinking how pretty a full-size quilt would be on a bed, with the borders making a flower garden all around. "Liberty Garden II" is the result. I used English paper piecing to make the hexagon rosettes and then machine appliquéd them onto the quilt. They also could be easily appliquéd with fusible web. Whichever appliqué method you choose, you are sure to have a garden blooming before you know it. The quilt diagram on page 36 shows block settings for various sizes.

FINISHED BLOCK SIZE: 18¾"

FINISHED QUILT SIZES

2 x 3 Blocks	3 x 3 Blocks	3 x 4 Blocks
66¼" x 88¾"	88¾" x 88¾"	88¾" x 111¼"

MATERIALS: 42"-WIDE FABRIC

Fabric	2 x 3 Blocks	3 x 3 Blocks	3 x 4 Blocks
White (block backgrounds, sashing, inner border)	5⅞ yards	7¼ yards	9½ yards
Green (blocks, outer border, appliqués, binding)	4 yards	4½ yards	5¼ yards
Medium pink floral (appliqués)	⅞ yard	1⅛ yards	1⅜ yards
Yellow floral #1 (appliqués)	⅝ yard	⅝ yard	1⅜ yards
Yellow floral #2 (appliqués)	½ yard	½ yard	⅝ yard
Medium blue floral (appliqués)	¾ yard	1 yard	1¼ yards
Dark blue (appliqués)	⅛ yard	⅛ yard	⅛ yard
Dark pink (appliqués)	⅛ yard	⅛ yard	⅛ yard
Medium green (appliqués)	⅛ yard	⅛ yard	⅛ yard
Backing	5½ yards	8¾ yards	9¾ yards
Batting	72" x 95"	95" x 95"	95" x 117"
Template plastic			
Freezer paper			

LIBERTY GARDEN, by Elizabeth Hamby Carlson, 1997, Montgomery Village, Maryland, 40" x 40". This small-scale quilt made with Liberty of London fabrics was the inspiration for the full-size "Liberty Garden II."

CUTTING STRIPS

Cut the required number of strips in the sizes indicated to make the quilt size you have chosen. Cut all strips across the full width of the fabric, selvage to selvage. All measurements include ¼"-wide seam allowances. Refer to "Cutting Straight Strips" (page 8) for additional guidance as needed.

NUMBER AND WIDTH OF STRIPS

Fabric	Cut Width	2 x 3 Blocks	3 x 3 Blocks	3 x 4 Blocks
Green	1¾"	16	17	23
	3"	4	4	6
White	1¾"	18	19	26
	3"	15	18	24
	4¼"	9	14	19
	6¾"	2	2	3

LIBERTY GARDEN II

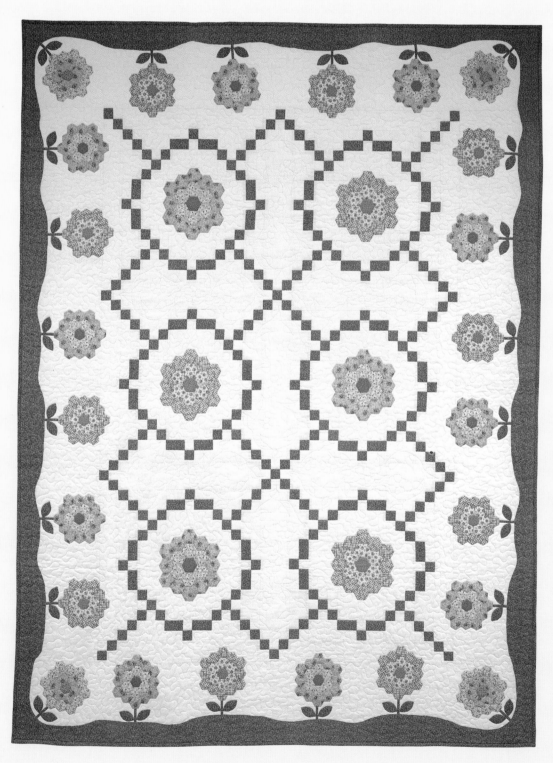

By Elizabeth Hamby Carlson, 2003, Montgomery Village, Maryland, 66¼" x 88¾". Quilted by Sheri Flemming.

Making the Block Units

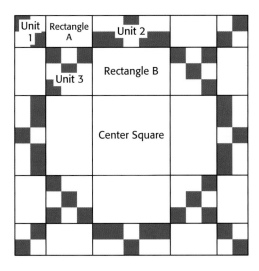

The pieced Liberty Garden block is made up of three units, two different sizes of background rectangles, and a center square. The units and rectangles are the same in each block. Follow the step-by-step instructions to make each unit, referring to the chart to find the number of units required for the size quilt you have chosen. The cutting instructions for the background rectangles and center square will be given later.

UNIT REQUIREMENTS

Unit	2 x 3 Blocks	3 x 3 Blocks	3 x 4 Blocks
One*	28	40	52
Two	24	36	48
Three	24	36	48

*Four of these will be set aside for the outer corners of the sashing.

Unit 1

1. Make the required number of strip sets, using one green and one white 1¾"-wide strip per set. Refer to "Making Strip Sets" on page 10 as needed.

NUMBER OF STRIP SETS

2 x 3 Blocks	3 x 3 Blocks	3 x 4 Blocks
3	4	5

2. Crosscut the strip sets into the required number of 1¾"-wide segments for the quilt size you are making. Refer to "Crosscutting Strip Sets" (page 10) for guidance.

NUMBER OF SEGMENTS

2 x 3 Blocks	3 x 3 Blocks	3 x 4 Blocks
56	80	104

3. Stitch two segments together as shown to make unit 1.

Unit 1

Unit 2

1. Make strip sets for rows 1 and 2 as shown, using two white or green 3"-wide strips and one green or white 1¾"-wide strip per set.

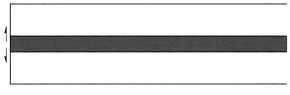

Row 1

Row 2

NUMBER OF STRIP SETS
(Make this number for each row.)

2 x 3 Blocks	3 x 3 Blocks	3 x 4 Blocks
2	2	3

2. Crosscut the strip sets into 1¾"-wide segments. Cut one segment from both the row 1 and row 2 strip sets for each unit 2 required.

3. Sew one row 1 segment and one row 2 segment together as shown to make unit 2.

Unit 2

Unit 3

1. Make strip sets for rows 1, 2, and 3 as shown, using the green and white 1¾"-wide strips.

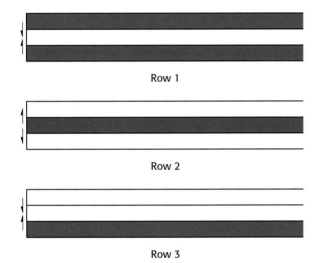

Row 1

Row 2

Row 3

NUMBER OF STRIP SETS
(Make this number for each row.)

2 x 3 Blocks	3 x 3 Blocks	3 x 4 Blocks
2	2	3

2. Crosscut the strip sets into 1¾"-wide segments. Cut one segment from the row 1, 2, and 3 strip sets for each unit 3 required.

3. Sew one each of the row 1, 2, and 3 segments together as shown to make unit 3.

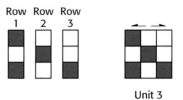

Unit 3

CUTTING THE BACKGROUND RECTANGLES AND CENTER SQUARES

Crosscut the required number of rectangles and squares in the sizes shown from the white strips.

NUMBER OF RECTANGLES AND SQUARES

Rectangle A

Strip Width	Cut Size	2 x 3 Blocks	3 x 3 Blocks	3 x 4 Blocks
3"	3" x 4¼"	48	72	96

Rectangle B

Strip Width	Cut Size	2 x 3 Blocks	3 x 3 Blocks	3 x 4 Blocks
4¼"	4¼" x 6¾"	24	36	48

Center Square

Strip Width	Cut Size	2 x 3 Blocks	3 x 3 Blocks	3 x 4 Blocks
6¾"	6¾" x 6¾"	6	9	12

Assembling the Blocks

1. Arrange the units, rectangles, and square into rows as shown. Stitch the pieces in each row together. Press seams in the directions indicated. Sew the rows together. Press the seams in the directions indicated. You will have four extra unit 1 units. Set these aside for the sashing corner blocks.

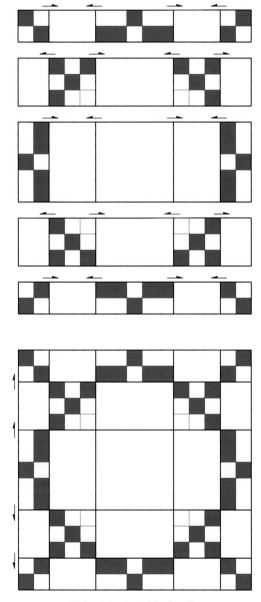

Make 6 for 2 x 3 block quilt.
Make 9 for 3 x 3 block quilt.
Make 12 for 3 x 4 block quilt.

2. To appliqué the blocks, trace the block hexagon on page 37 onto template plastic. Cut out the template with a utility knife and straightedge, rather than with scissors, to ensure accuracy. Using the template, trace the shape onto freezer paper 19 times for each block in your quilt. Cut out the freezer-paper shapes.

3. Refer to the quilt diagram on page 36 to determine the number of blocks with pink flowers and the number of blocks with blue flowers. Using a hot, dry iron, press the freezer-paper shapes, shiny side down, to the wrong side of the appropriate fabrics, leaving at least ½" between shapes. For *each* block with a pink flower, press 12 shapes onto the medium pink fabric for the flower outer ring, 6 shapes onto the yellow #1 fabric for the flower inner ring, and 1 shape onto the dark pink fabric for the flower center. Repeat for the blue flowers, using medium blue for the flower outer rings, yellow #2 for the flower inner rings, and dark blue for the flower centers. Cut out each shape, adding a ¼" seam allowance all around.

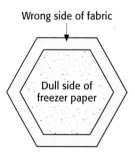

Wrong side of fabric

Dull side of freezer paper

4. Fold the seam allowance over each paper shape and baste it in place through all the layers. Fold one side at a time to keep the corners crisp.

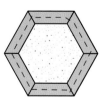

5. Arrange the shapes to form the rosettes, referring to the photo if necessary. Working from the center out and following the diagram for stitching sequence, place the right sides of two hexagons together. Join them with tiny whipstitches, catching just a few threads at the edge of each hexagon.

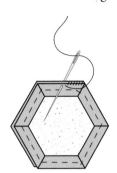

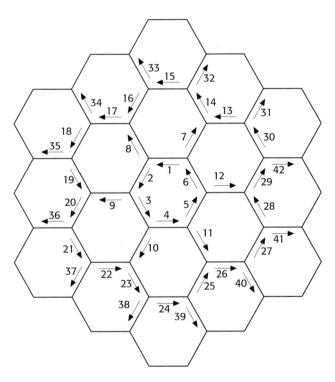

6. Press the finished rosettes firmly. Using spray starch when pressing will help maintain the sharp, creased edges after the papers are removed, making the rosettes easier to appliqué to the blocks. Carefully remove the basting threads and papers.

7. Center a rosette on each pieced block and pin or baste it securely in place. Appliqué the edges of the rosette to the block. If desired, trim the background fabric from behind the rosettes.

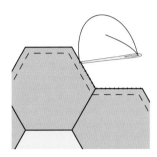

Making the Sashing

1. Crosscut the required number of strips from the white 3"- and 4¼"-wide strips.

NUMBER OF SASHING STRIPS

Strip Width	Sashing Dimensions	2 x 3 Blocks	3 x 3 Blocks	3 x 4 Blocks
4¼"	4¼" x 19¼"	7	12	17
3"	3" x 19¼"	10	12	14

2. Make one strip set *each* for rows 1 and 2 of the center and side sashing blocks as shown, using the green and white 1¾"-wide strips.

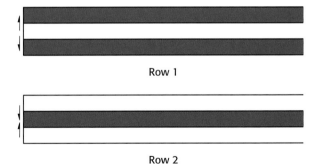

Row 1

Row 2

3. Crosscut the strip sets into 1¾"-wide segments.

NUMBER OF SEGMENTS

Row	2 x 3 Blocks	3 x 3 Blocks	3 x 4 Blocks
1	10	16	22
2	8	12	16

4. For each block, arrange the segments into rows as shown. Stitch the rows together.

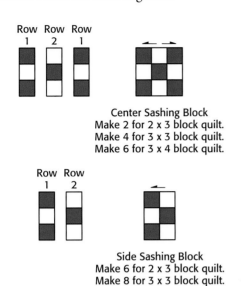

Center Sashing Block
Make 2 for 2 x 3 block quilt.
Make 4 for 3 x 3 block quilt.
Make 6 for 3 x 4 block quilt.

Side Sashing Block
Make 6 for 2 x 3 block quilt.
Make 8 for 3 x 3 block quilt.
Make 10 for 3 x 4 block quilt.

ASSEMBLING THE QUILT TOP

1. Refer to the quilt diagram on page 36 to arrange the appliquéd blocks, the sashing rectangles, and the sashing blocks into horizontal rows. Note that the sashing rectangles in the center of the quilt top are 4¼" wide; the rectangles on the outside are 3" wide. The placement of the sashing blocks for the 2 x 3 and 3 x 3 quilt plans will need to be changed slightly from the diagram shown so that the corner sashing blocks are in each corner and the side sashing blocks are positioned along the outside of the quilt top with the row 2 segments toward the outside of the quilt. Stitch the pieces in each row together. Press the seams toward the sashing rectangles. Carefully pin the rows together to match seams. Sew the rows together. Press the seams toward the sashing rows.

2. Referring to "Straight-Cut Borders" (page 12), cut 10½"-wide border strips from the white fabric and sew them to the quilt.

3. To make the freezer-paper templates for marking the curved border, cut a piece of freezer paper the same width and length as the top border of your quilt. Referring to the diagram below, draw a line 10¼" from each end of the piece to mark the corner squares. From each of the drawn lines, measure 23¾" and draw another line. For quilt arrangements that are two blocks wide the line will be in the center of the border. For quilt arrangements that are three blocks wide, the distance between the lines should be 22½".

4. Enlarge the border corner pattern on page 37 onto paper or cardboard. Place the corner template in each corner of the freezer-paper template from step 3 so that the curve is toward the center of the quilt top; trace around it. Refer to the illustration

Two-Block-Wide Quilt Arrangement

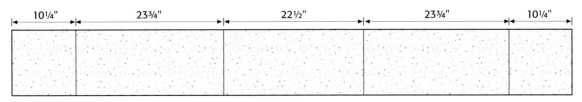

Three-Block-Wide Quilt Arrangement

below and to the photo on page 28 to draw a gently curved line onto each of the remaining sections of the pieces, making sure that the high and low points are no higher or lower than those indicated.

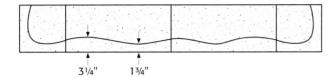

5. Cut out the top border freezer-paper template on the curved line.

6. Make a freezer-paper border template for the side borders in the same manner, eliminating the corner squares.

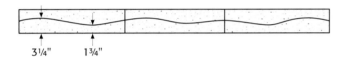

7. Cut the outer border strips from the green fabric.

BORDER STRIPS

Block Arrangement	Number and Size of Strips
2 x 3 Blocks	2 strips, 10½" x 66¾", for top and bottom borders
	2 strips, 5" x 69¼", for side borders
3 x 3 Blocks	2 strips, 10½" x 89¼", for top and bottom borders
	2 strips, 5" x 69¼", for side borders
3 x 4 Blocks	2 strips, 10½" x 89¼", for top and bottom borders
	2 strips, 5" x 91¾", for side borders

8. Using a hot, dry iron, press the top border freezer-paper template, shiny side down, onto the green top border strip, matching center points and aligning the long, straight edge of the template with the outer edge of the border strip. With a sharp pencil, trace the curved edge of the template onto the fabric. Remove the freezer-paper template and use it to mark the remaining border strip of the same length. Use the side border freezer-paper templates to mark the side border strips in the same manner.

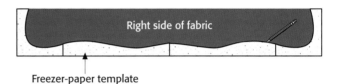

Freezer-paper template

9. Place the marked green outer side border strips over the white inner side borders, right sides up, matching centers and aligning outer edges. To keep both borders aligned during stitching, pin the borders in place, and then baste about ¼" inside the drawn line of the green border and along the outer edges. Repeat with the top and bottom borders, folding the ends over the side borders where they meet; baste in place.

Basting

10. Beginning at one end, trim the green border fabric 3/16" from the drawn line. Be careful not to cut the white inner border at the same time!

11. Refer to the quilt diagram on page 36 to pencil-mark the flower-stem placement lines on the border.

Stem placement line

12. To make the stems, cut 1"-wide bias strips from the green fabric. Cut a 2" length of bias for each stem. Be careful that you do not cut all of the green fabric into bias strips because you still need to cut out the leaves and binding.

13. Press each bias strip in half, wrong sides together. Center a strip on each placement line on the border. Make sure one end of each strip extends under the green border. Stitch the stems to the placement line by hand with a small running stitch or by machine with a straight machine

stitch. Press the strip folded edges over the stitching and appliqué the loose edge in place.

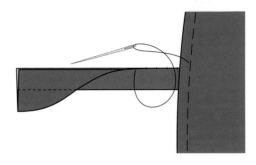

14. Appliqué the outer border to the inner border, turning under the seam allowance with your needle as you go. Turn just a little bit at a time on curves, using a sweeping motion to smooth the seam allowance underneath. Appliqué the overlapped ends of the outer top and bottom borders to the side borders to finish the edges.

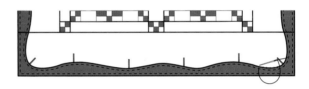

15. When the green border is completely appliquéd, remove the basting. Turn the quilt over and trim the inner border fabric behind the outer border fabric to within ¼" of the appliquéd edge.

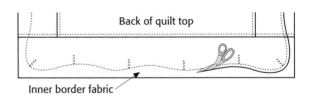

Back of quilt top

Inner border fabric

16. Trace the leaf template on page 37 onto template plastic and cut it out. Using the template, make two freezerpaper shapes for each stem. Press the shapes onto the wrong side of the remaining green fabric, leaving at least ½" of additional space all around. Cut out each leaf, adding a ¼" seam allowance. Appliqué a leaf to each side of each stem.

17. Trace the border hexagon template on page 37 onto template plastic and cut it out. Referring to the quilt diagram below and following steps 2–6 of "Assembling the Blocks," determine the amount of pink and blue rosettes and make them in the same manner as the block rosettes, using the border hexagon template. In addition, you will need four corner rosettes. Make the outer ring from the yellow #1 fabric, the inner ring from the medium pink fabric, and the center from the medium green fabric. Pin or baste the rosettes to the top of each stem and appliqué them in place.

FINISHING

Refer to "Backing and Batting" (page 13), "Layering and Basting" (page 14), "Quilting" (page 14), and "Binding" (page 14) as needed.

1. Piece the quilt backing as necessary. Center the quilt top and batting over the backing; baste.

2. Quilt as desired.

3. Trim the backing and batting. Cut the binding fabric into 2½"-wide bias strips. Sew the binding to the quilt.

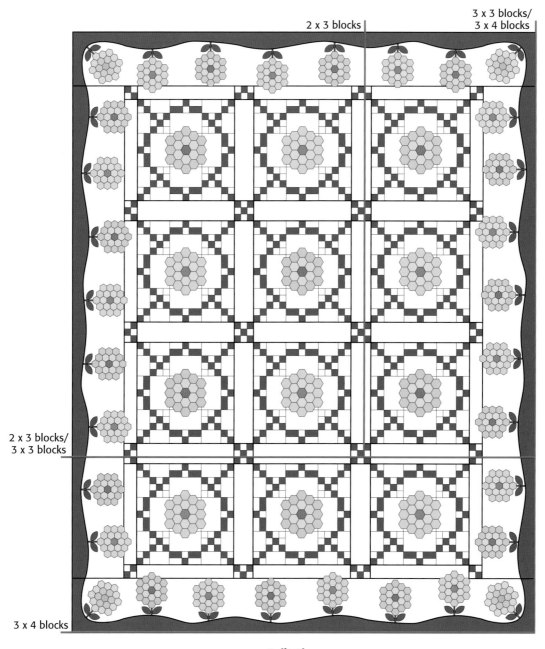

Quilt Diagram

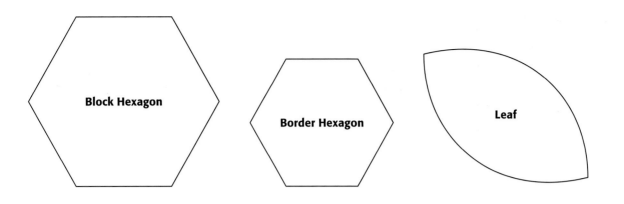

Block Hexagon

Border Hexagon

Leaf

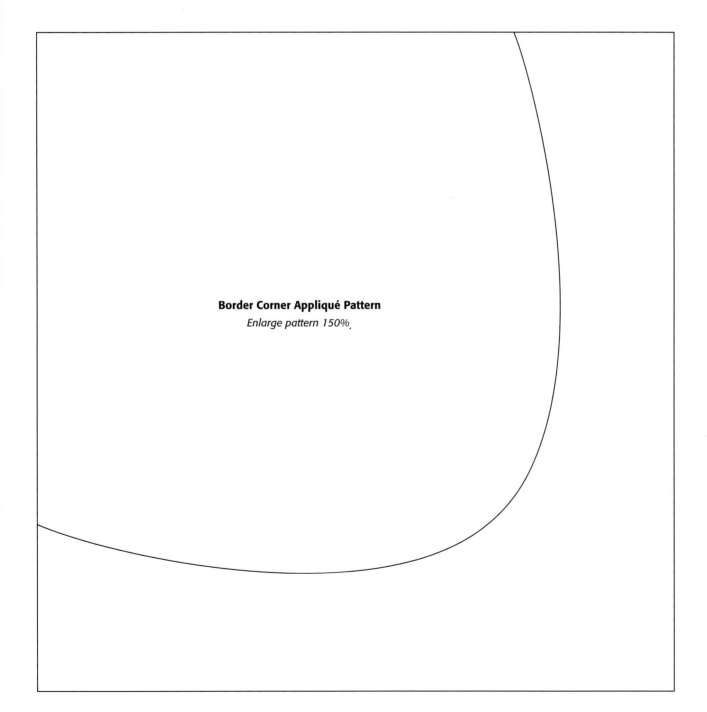

Border Corner Appliqué Pattern
Enlarge pattern 150%.

FAT QUARTER FANCY

Here is your chance to make a scrappy Burgoyne Surrounded using your collection of fat quarters. Be sure to select a background color that provides a value contrast to the fat quarters and defines the pieced design. Two block sizes and three setting options are given for making the quilt in various sizes. Select a block size, refer to the corresponding columns in the charts to make block units in that size, and then arrange the finished blocks according to the diagram on page 46.

FINISHED BLOCK SIZES (Choose one.)

Block	Block Size
A	15"
B	18¾"

FINISHED QUILT SIZES

Block	2 x 3 Blocks	3 x 3 Blocks	3 x 4 Blocks
A	39" x 57"	57" x 57"	57" x 75"
B	48¾" x 71¼"	71¼" x 71¼"	71¼" x 93¾"

MATERIALS: 42"-WIDE FABRIC

Block A

Fabric	2 x 3 Blocks	3 x 3 Blocks	3 x 4 Blocks
Dark fat quarters (blocks, sashing)	6 minimum	8 minimum	10 minimum
Light fat quarters (block backgrounds, sashing)	11 minimum	15 minimum	20 minimum
Backing	3½ yards	3½ yards	4⅝ yards
Binding	⅞ yard	⅞ yard	1 yard
Batting	45" x 63"	63" x 63"	63" x 81"

Block B

Fabric	2 x 3 Blocks	3 x 3 Blocks	3 x 4 Blocks
Dark fat quarters (blocks, sashing)	7 minimum	9 minimum	12 minimum
Light fat quarters (block backgrounds, sashing)	15 minimum	20 minimum	25 minimum
Backing	3¼ yards	4½ yards	5⅝ yards
Binding	⅞ yard	1 yard	1 yard
Batting	55" x 77"	77" x 77"	77" x 100"

CUTTING STRIPS

Cut the required number of strips in the appropriate width to make the quilt size you have chosen. Cut all strips across the full width (21") of the fat quarter unless directed otherwise. All measurements include ¼"-wide seam allowances. Refer to "Cutting Straight Strips" (page 8) for additional guidance as needed.

NUMBER AND WIDTH OF STRIPS

Block A

Fabric	Cut Width	2 x 3 Blocks	3 x 3 Blocks	3 x 4 Blocks
Dark fat quarters	1½"	49	69	90
Light fat quarters	1½"	64	88	114
	2½"	14	20	26
	5½"	5	8	10

Block B

Fabric	Cut Width	2 x 3 Blocks	3 x 3 Blocks	3 x 4 Blocks
Dark fat quarters	1¾"	57	80	105
Light fat quarters	1¾"	75	96	124
	3"	6	10	12
	4¼"	16	24	32

FAT QUARTER FANCY

By Elizabeth Hamby Carlson, 2003, Montgomery Village, Maryland, 57" x 57".

Making the Block Units

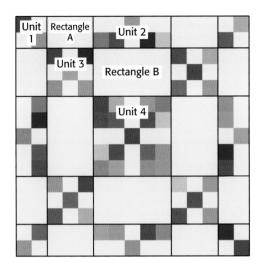

The fat-quarter Burgoyne Surrounded block is made up of four units and two different sizes of background rectangles. The units and rectangles are the same in each block. Follow the step-by-step instructions to make each unit, referring to the chart to find the number of units required for the size quilt you have chosen. Note that the number of units and rectangles required is the same for both block sizes. The cutting instructions for the background rectangles will be given later.

UNIT REQUIREMENTS

Unit	2 x 3 Blocks	3 x 3 Blocks	3 x 4 Blocks
One	24	36	48
Two	24	36	48
Three*	26	40	54
Four	6	9	12

Some of these units will be set aside and used later for the center sashing blocks.

Unit 1

1. Make the required number of strip sets for the quilt size you have chosen, using one light and one dark strip per set. For block A quilts, use 1½"-wide strips. For block B quilts, use 1¾"-wide strips. Refer to "Making Strip Sets" (page 10) as needed.

NUMBER OF STRIP SETS

Block	2 x 3 Blocks	3 x 3 Blocks	3 x 4 Blocks
A	4	6	8
B	5	7	9

2. Crosscut the strip sets into segments the same width as the strip width used to make the strip sets (1½" or 1¾"). Refer to "Crosscutting Strip Sets" (page 10) for guidance. Note that the number of segments to cut is the same for both block sizes.

NUMBER OF SEGMENTS

2 x 3 Blocks	3 x 3 Blocks	3 x 4 Blocks
48	72	96

3. Stitch two segments together as shown to make unit 1.

Unit 1

Unit 2

1. Make strip sets for rows 1 and 2 as shown. For block A quilts, use two dark 1½"-wide strips for row 1; for row 2 use two light 2½"-wide strips and one dark 1½"-wide strip. For block B quilts, use two dark 1¾"-wide strips for row 1; for row 2 use two light 3"-wide strips and one dark 1¾"-wide strip.

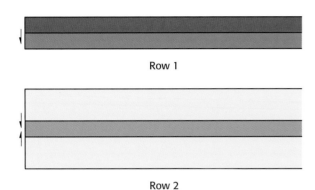

Row 1

Row 2

NUMBER OF STRIP SETS

Block	Row	2 x 3 Blocks	3 x 3 Blocks	3 x 4 Blocks
A	1	8	12	15
	2	3	4	5
B	1	9	14	18
	2	3	5	6

2. Crosscut the strip sets into segments the same width as the narrow strip width used to make the strip sets (1½" or 1¾"). Note that the number of segments to cut is the same for both block sizes.

NUMBER OF SEGMENTS

Row	2 x 3 Blocks	3 x 3 Blocks	3 x 4 Blocks
1	96	144	192
2	30	45	60

3. From light 1½"-wide strips (block A) or 1¾"-wide strips (block B), cut squares the same size as the strip width. Cut one square for each unit 2 required.

4. Stitch a row 1 segment to each side of each light square to complete row 1. Set the remaining row 1 segments aside for unit 4.

5. Sew one row 1 segment and one row 2 segment together as shown to make unit 2. Set the remaining row 2 segments aside for unit 4.

Unit 2

Unit 3

1. Make strip sets for rows 1 and 2 as shown, using the light and dark strips. For block A quilts, use 1½"-wide strips. For block B quilts, use 1¾"-wide strips.

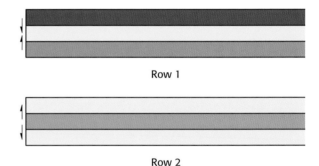

Row 1

Row 2

NUMBER OF STRIP SETS

Block	Row	2 x 3 Blocks	3 x 3 Blocks	3 x 4 Blocks
A	1	5	7	10
	2	3	4	6
B	1	6	8	11
	2	4	5	7

2. Crosscut the strip sets into segments the same width as the strip width used to make the strip sets (1½" or 1¾"). Note that the number of segments to cut is the same for both block sizes.

NUMBER OF SEGMENTS

Row	2 x 3 Blocks	3 x 3 Blocks	3 x 4 Blocks
1	58	88	118
2	36	52	68

3. Sew two row 1 segments and one row 2 segment together as shown to make the required number of unit 3 units. Set aside the remaining segments for the sashing blocks.

Unit 3

Unit 4

1. Using the unit 2 row 1 segments that you previously set aside, stitch two segments together as shown to make a four-patch unit.

2. From light 1½"-wide strips (block A) or 1¾"-wide strips (block B), cut two rectangles for each unit 4 in your quilt. For block A quilts, cut the rectangles 1½" x 2½". For block B quilts, cut the rectangles 1¾" x 3".

3. Assemble the four-patch units, the light rectangles, and the unit 2 row 2 segments that you previously set aside as shown. Stitch the units in each row together. Then stitch the rows together.

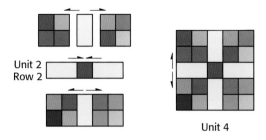

Unit 2
Row 2

Unit 4

CUTTING THE BACKGROUND RECTANGLES

Crosscut the light 2½"-wide strips (block A) or 4¼"-wide strips (block B) into background rectangle A. For block A quilts, cut the rectangles 2½" x 3". For block B quilts, cut the rectangles 3" x 4¼". Crosscut the light 5½"-wide strips (block A) or 4¼"-wide strips (block B) into background rectangle B. For block A quilts, cut the rectangles 3½" x 5½". For block B quilts, cut the rectangles 4¼" x 6¾". For block B quilts, follow the cutting plan shown to use the least amount of strips. Note that the number to cut is the same for both block sizes.

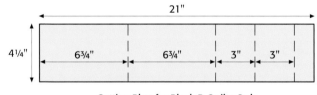

Cutting Plan for Block B Quilts Only

RECTANGLE CUTTING

Rectangle	2 x 3 Blocks	3 x 3 Blocks	3 x 4 Blocks
A	48	72	96
B	24	36	48

ASSEMBLING THE BLOCKS

Arrange the units and rectangles into rows as shown. Stitch the units and rectangles in each row together. Press the seams in the directions indicated. Sew the rows together. Press the seams in the directions indicated. Set aside the remaining unit 3 units for the center sashing blocks.

TIP: Use a design wall or flannel board to arrange the fabric placement for each block before sewing the pieces together.

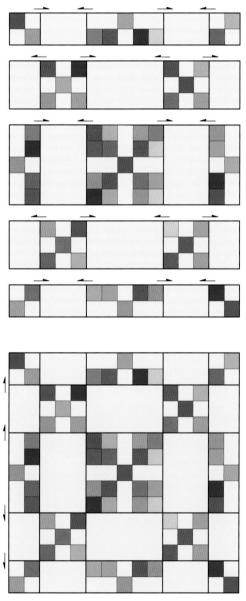

Make 6 for 2 x 3 block quilt.
Make 9 for 3 x 3 block quilt.
Make 12 for 3 x 4 block quilt.

MAKING THE SASHING

1. Crosscut the required number of strips from the light 1½"-wide strips (block A) or 1¾"-wide strips (block B) for the top and bottom of the pieced sashing strips. For block A quilts, cut the strips 1½" x 15½". From the remainder of the strips, cut the required number of 1½" squares. For block B quilts, cut the strips 1¾" x 19¼". From the remainder of the strips, cut the required number of squares. Note that the number of sashing strips is the same for both block sizes.

NUMBER OF SASHING STRIPS

Piece	2 x 3 Blocks	3 x 3 Blocks	3 x 4 Blocks
Sashing strips	34	48	62
Squares	51	72	93

FAT QUARTER FANCY by Dolores A. Pilla, 2003, Fayetteville, Pennsylvania, 79¼" x 79¼". Quilted by Leah Richard. Dolores used her collection of reproduction-fabric fat quarters to make this beautiful quilt. The softly striped border finishes it off perfectly.

2. Make strip sets 1, 2, and 3 as shown for the center of the pieced sashing strips and the side and corner sashing blocks, using the light and dark 1½"-wide strips (block A) or 1¾"-wide strips (block B).

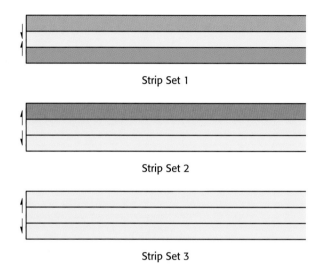

Strip Set 1

Strip Set 2

Strip Set 3

NUMBER OF STRIP SETS

Block	Strip Set	2 x 3 Blocks	3 x 3 Blocks	3 x 4 Blocks
A	1	6	8	10
	2	1	1	1
	3	1	1	1
B	1	7	9	12
	2	1	1	1
	3	1	1	1

3. Crosscut the strip sets into segments the same width as the strip width used to make the strip sets (1½" or 1¾"). Note that the number of segments to cut is the same for both block sizes.

NUMBER OF SEGMENTS

Strip Set	2 x 3 Blocks	3 x 3 Blocks	3 x 4 Blocks
1	68	96	124
2	8	8	8
3	6	8	10

4. Make the number of pieced-center sashing strips required for the quilt size you are making. To make each strip, alternately sew four strip-set 1 segments together with three of the light squares you cut in step 1 as shown. Note that the number to make is the same for both block sizes.

NUMBER OF PIECED-CENTER SASHING STRIPS

2 x 3 Blocks	3 x 3 Blocks	3 x 4 Blocks
17	24	31

5. Sew a sashing rectangle from step 1 to each side of the pieced-center sashing strips as shown.

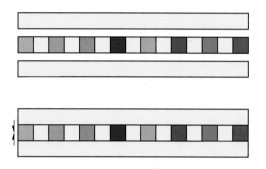

6. To make the side and corner sashing blocks, arrange the remaining unit 3 row 1 and 2 segments and the strip set 2 and 3 segments into rows as shown. Stitch the rows together.

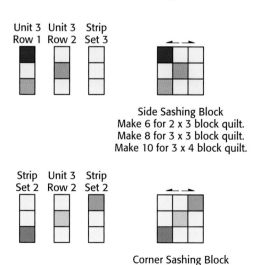

Unit 3 Unit 3 Strip
Row 1 Row 2 Set 3

Side Sashing Block
Make 6 for 2 x 3 block quilt.
Make 8 for 3 x 3 block quilt.
Make 10 for 3 x 4 block quilt.

Strip Unit 3 Strip
Set 2 Row 2 Set 2

Corner Sashing Block
Make 4 for all quilt sizes.

ASSEMBLING THE QUILT TOP

Refer to the quilt diagram to arrange the fat-quarter Burgoyne Surrounded blocks, the pieced sashing strips, and the sashing blocks into horizontal rows. The placement of the sashing blocks for the 2 x 3 and 3 x 3 quilt plans will need to be changed slightly from the diagram shown so that the corner sashing blocks are in each corner and the side sashing blocks are positioned along the outside of the quilt top with the strip set 3 segments toward the outside of the quilt. Stitch the pieces in each row together. Press the seams toward the sashing strips. Carefully pin the rows together to match seams. Sew the rows together. Press the seams toward the sashing rows.

FINISHING

Refer to "Backing and Batting" (page 13), "Layering and Basting" (page 14), "Quilting" (page 14), and "Binding" (page 14) as needed.

1. Piece the quilt backing as necessary. Center the quilt top and batting over the backing; baste.

2. Quilt as desired.

3. Trim the backing and batting. Cut the binding fabric into 2½"-wide bias strips. Sew the binding to the quilt.

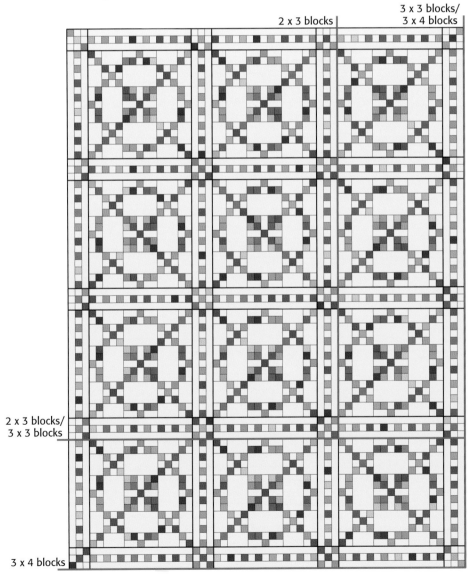

Quilt Diagram

STARS
SURROUNDED

Multifabric Sawtooth Star blocks enhance this patriotic
red-white-and-blue quilt. Pieced sashing strips and a
bright border add color and flair. The quilt diagram on
page 56 indicates setting options for making the quilt in
various sizes.

STARS SURROUNDED

By Elizabeth Hamby Carlson, 2003, Montgomery Village, Maryland, 74" x 74". Quilted by Leah Richard.

FINISHED BLOCK SIZE: 17"

FINISHED QUILT SIZES

2 x 3 Blocks	3 x 3 Blocks	3 x 4 Blocks
54" x 74"	74" x 74"	74" x 94"

MATERIALS: 42"-WIDE FABRIC

Fabric	2 x 3 Blocks	3 x 3 Blocks	3 x 4 Blocks
White (block backgrounds)	3⅛ yards	4½ yards	5⅝ yards
Red (blocks, sashing, border, binding)	3¾ yards	4½ yards	5 yards
Blue (blocks)	¾ yard	1 yard	1⅜ yards
Tan (blocks)	⅜ yard	½ yard	⅝ yard
Gold (blocks, sashing)	¼ yard	¼ yard	¼ yard
Assorted reds (block center units)	⅛ yard or 6" square for *each* block (6)	⅛ yard or 6" square for *each* block (9)	⅛ yard or 6" square for *each* block (12)
Assorted blues (block center units)	⅛ yard or 6" square for *each* block (6)	⅛ yard or 6" square for *each* block (9)	⅛ yard or 6" square for *each* block (12)
Assorted light neutrals (block center units)	⅛ yard or 8" square for *each* block (6)	⅛ yard or 8" square for *each* block (9)	⅛ yard or 8" square for *each* block (12)
Assorted golds (block center units)	⅛ yard or 8" square for *each* block (6)	⅛ yard or 8" square for *each* block (9)	⅛ yard or 8" square for *each* block (12)
Backing	4⅝ yards	4⅝ yards	6 yards
Batting	60" x 80"	80" x 80"	80" x 100"

CUTTING STRIPS

Cut the required number of strips in the appropriate width to make the quilt size you have chosen. Cut all strips across the full width of the fabric, selvage to selvage. All measurements include ¼"-wide seam allowances. Refer to "Cutting Straight Strips" (page 8) for additional guidance as needed.

NUMBER AND WIDTH OF STRIPS

Fabric	Cut Width	2 x 3 Blocks	3 x 3 Blocks	3 x 4 Blocks
White	1¼"	3	4	4
	1⅜"	5	7	9
	1½"	34	49	62
	2½"	10	15	19
	3½"	4	6	8
Red	1⅜"	1	2	2
	1½"	14	20	25
	2"	1	1	1
Blue	1½"	4	6	8
	3½"	4	6	8
Tan	1½"	5	8	10
Gold	1¼"	2	3	3

MAKING THE BLOCK UNITS

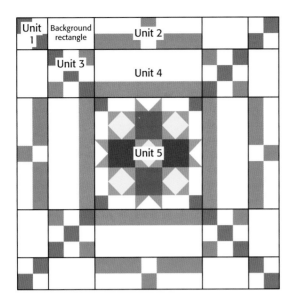

The Stars Surrounded block is made up of five units and one background rectangle. Units 1 through 4 and the rectangles are the same in each block. Unit 5's construction is the same in each block, but the fabrics in each block vary. Follow the step-by-step instructions to make each unit, referring to the chart to find the number of units required for the size quilt you have chosen. The cutting instructions for the background rectangle will be given later.

UNIT REQUIREMENTS

Unit	2 x 3 Blocks	3 x 3 Blocks	3 x 4 Blocks
One	24	36	48
Two	24	36	48
Three	24	36	48
Four	24	36	48
Five	6	9	12

Unit 1

1. Make the required number of strip sets, using one red and one white 1½"-wide strip. Refer to "Making Strip Sets" on page 10 as needed.

NUMBER OF STRIP SETS

2 x 3 Blocks	3 x 3 Blocks	3 x 4 Blocks
2	3	4

2. Crosscut the strip sets into the required number of 1½"-wide segments for the quilt size you are making. Refer to "Crosscutting Strip Sets" (page 10) for guidance.

NUMBER OF SEGMENTS

2 x 3 Blocks	3 x 3 Blocks	3 x 4 Blocks
48	72	96

3. Stitch two segments together as shown to make unit 1.

Unit 1

Unit 2

1. Make strip sets for rows 1 and 2 as shown, using two white or blue 3½"-wide strips and one white or blue 1½"-wide strip per set.

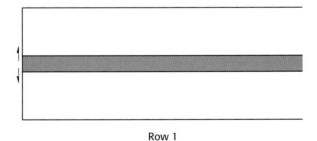

Row 1

Row 2

NUMBER OF STRIP SETS
(Make this number for each row.)

2 x 3 Blocks	3 x 3 Blocks	3 x 4 Blocks
2	3	4

2. Crosscut the strip sets into 1½"-wide segments. Cut one segment from both the row 1 and row 2 strip sets for each unit 2 required.

3. Sew one row 1 segment and one row 2 segment together as shown to make unit 2.

Unit 2

Unit 3

1. Make strip sets for rows 1 and 2 as shown, using the red, white, and blue 1½"-wide strips.

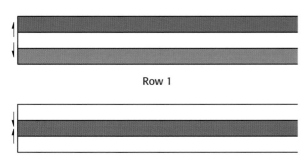

Row 1

Row 2

NUMBER OF STRIP SETS

Row	2 x 3 Blocks	3 x 3 Blocks	3 x 4 Blocks
1	2	3	4
2	1	2	2

2. Crosscut the strip sets into 1½"-wide segments.

NUMBER OF SEGMENTS

Row	2 x 3 Blocks	3 x 3 Blocks	3 x 4 Blocks
1	48	72	96
2	24	36	48

3. Sew two row 1 segments and one row 2 segment together as shown to make unit 3.

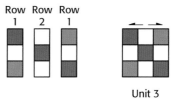

Unit 3

Unit 4

1. Make the required number of strip sets, using one tan 1½"-wide strip and one white 2½"-wide strip.

NUMBER OF STRIP SETS

2 x 3 Blocks	3 x 3 Blocks	3 x 4 Blocks
5	8	10

2. Crosscut the strip sets into 7½"-wide segments. Cut one segment for each unit 4 required.

Unit 5

1. Crosscut the required number of squares from the red 1⅜"-wide strips and the required number of rectangles from the white 1⅜"-wide strips.

NUMBER OF SQUARES AND RECTANGLES

Fabric	Cut Size	2 x 3 Blocks	3 x 3 Blocks	3 x 4 Blocks
Red	1⅜" x 1⅜"	24	36	48
White	1⅜" x 2¼"	72	108	144

2. For *each* unit 5 required for the quilt size you are making, cut the following pieces from one of the assorted red, assorted blue, assorted light neutral, and assorted gold fabrics. Use different fabrics in each of the units to give the quilt more visual interest and texture.

ADDITIONAL CUTTING REQUIREMENTS
(Cut this number for each unit 5 required.)

Fabric	Number and Size to Cut
Assorted red	2 squares, 2¼" x 2¼"
Assorted blue	2 squares, 2¼" x 2¼"
Assorted light neutral	5 squares, 2¼" x 2¼"
Assorted gold	28 squares, 1⅜" x 1⅜"

3. Draw a diagonal line on the wrong side of each gold square, using a sharp pencil or permanent-ink pen.

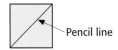

Pencil line

4. Place matching gold squares on opposite corners of a light neutral 2¼" square as shown, right sides together and raw edges even. Using the drawn lines as a guide, stitch a needle's width outside each line. The edge of the needle should just touch the line.

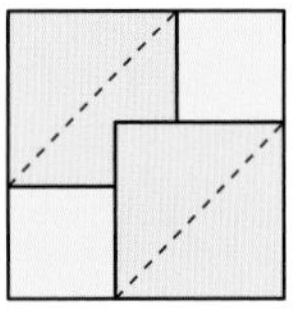

5. Trim the seam allowances to ⅛". Press the gold pieces away from the square, forming two new corners for the square.

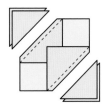

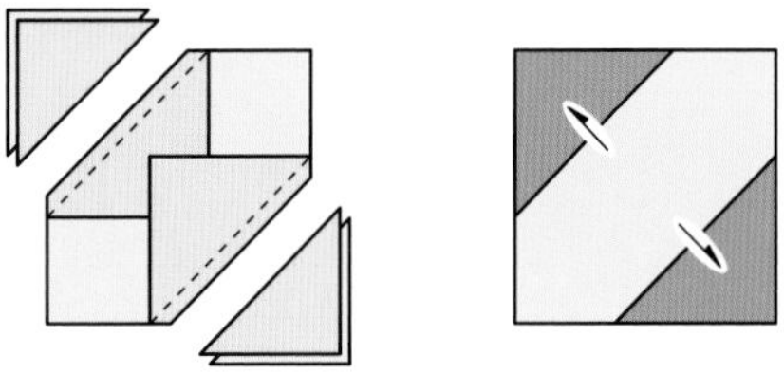

6. Repeat for the remaining two corners of the square.

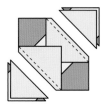

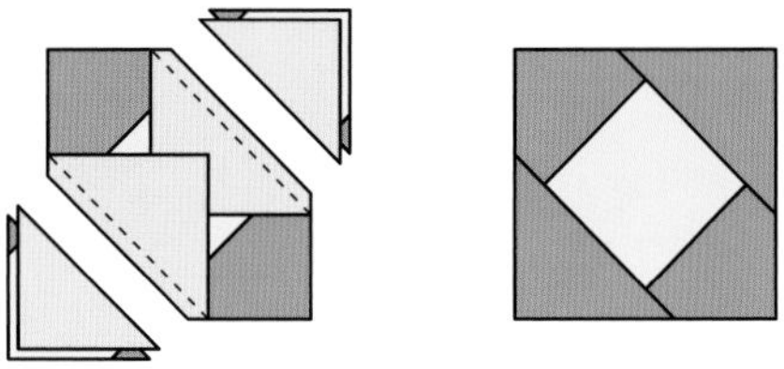

7. Repeat steps 4–6 with each light neutral square, using the same gold squares for each different light neutral square.

8. Place a gold square on one end of each white 1⅜" x 2¼" rectangle as shown, right sides together and raw edges even. Refer to steps 4 and 5 to stitch on the diagonal line and trim and press the piece.

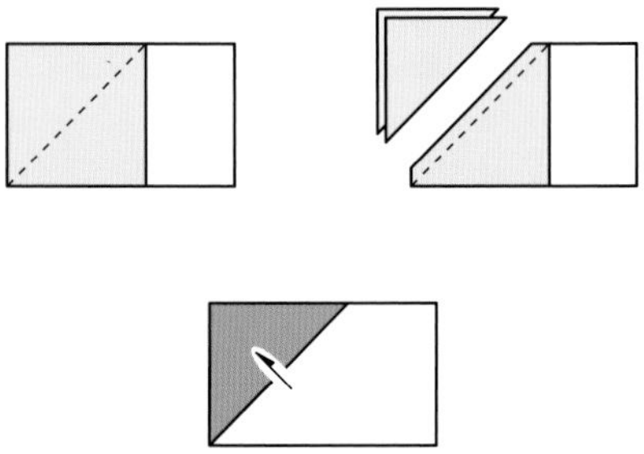

9. Using a matching gold square, repeat for the remaining end of each rectangle.

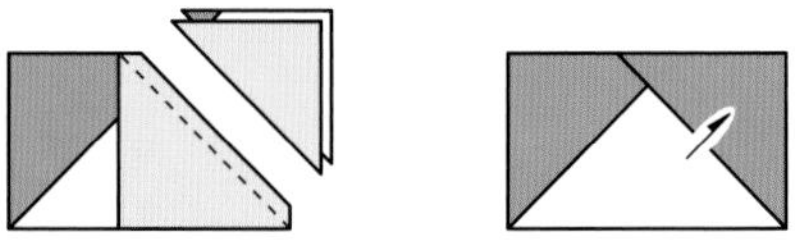

10. Arrange the unit pieces into rows as shown, being sure that the gold in the pieced units and the red and blue 2¼" squares are the same within each unit. Stitch the pieces in each row together, and then stitch the rows together to complete unit 5.

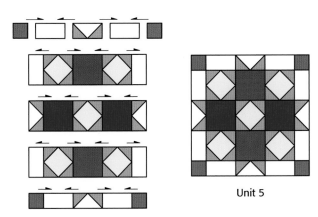

Unit 5

TIP: The stitching lines on the back of the pieced squares and rectangles cross to form an X. For a perfect point when sewing these pieces to another piece, your stitching line should go through the center of the X.

CUTTING THE BACKGROUND RECTANGLES

Crosscut the white 2½"-wide strips into 2½" x 3½" background rectangles.

NUMBER OF RECTANGLES

2 x 3 Blocks	3 x 3 Blocks	3 x 4 Blocks
48	72	96

ASSEMBLING THE BLOCKS

Arrange the units and background rectangles into rows as shown. Stitch the pieces in each row together. Press the seams in the directions indicated. Sew the rows together. Press the seams in the directions indicated.

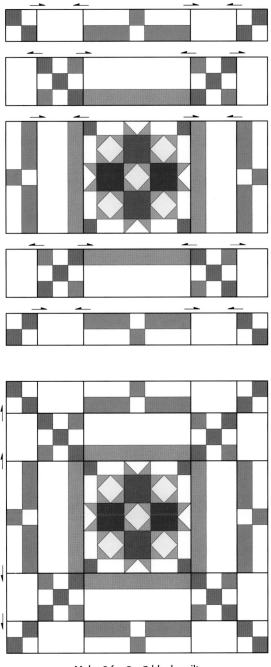

Make 6 for 2 x 3 block quilt.
Make 9 for 3 x 3 block quilt.
Make 12 for 3 x 4 block quilt.

MAKING THE SASHING

1. Crosscut the required number of 1½" x 17½" strips from the white 1½"-wide strips. Using the leftovers of each strip, cut one 1½" x 1½" square for *each* sashing strip cut.

NUMBER OF SASHING STRIPS

2 x 3 Blocks	3 x 3 Blocks	3 x 4 Blocks
34	48	62

2. Make strip sets for the center of the pieced sashing strips as shown, using the red and white 1½"-wide strips.

NUMBER OF STRIP SETS

2 x 3 Blocks	3 x 3 Blocks	3 x 4 Blocks
2	3	4

3. Crosscut the strip sets into 1½"-wide segments.

NUMBER OF SEGMENTS

2 x 3 Blocks	3 x 3 Blocks	3 x 4 Blocks
51	72	93

4. Make the number of pieced-center sashing strips required for the quilt size you are making. To make each strip, alternately sew three segments together with two of the white squares you cut in step 1 as shown.

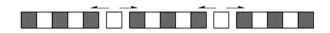

NUMBER OF PIECED-CENTER SASHING STRIPS

2 x 3 Blocks	3 x 3 Blocks	3 x 4 Blocks
17	24	31

5. Sew a sashing rectangle from step 1 to each side of the pieced-center sashing strips as shown.

6. To make the side sashing blocks, use the red and white 1½"-wide strips to make one strip set *each* of row 1 and row 2 as shown.

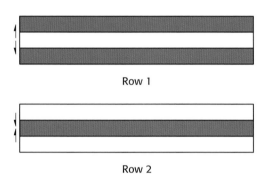

Row 1

Row 2

7. Crosscut *each* strip set into the required number of 1½"-wide segments for the quilt size you are making. Cut the same number of 1½" x 3½" rectangles from the white 1½"-wide strips.

NUMBER OF SEGMENTS AND RECTANGLES

2 x 3 Blocks	3 x 3 Blocks	3 x 4 Blocks
6	8	10

8. Arrange one row 1 segment, one row 2 segment, and one rectangle as shown to make the side sashing blocks.

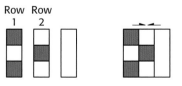

Row Row
1   2

Make 6 for 2 x 3 block quilt.
Make 8 for 3 x 3 block quilt.
Make 10 for 3 x 4 block quilt.

9. To make the star sashing blocks, refer to the chart below to cut the required number of squares and rectangles in the sizes shown from the white, gold, and red strips.

CUTTING FOR STAR SASHING BLOCK

Fabric	Strip Width	Cut Size	2 x 3 Blocks	3 x 3 Blocks	3 x 4 Blocks
White	1¼"	1¼" x 1¼"	24	32	40
	1¼"	1¼" x 2"	24	32	40
Gold	1¼"	1¼" x 1¼"	48	64	80
Red	2"	2" x 2"	6	8	10

10. Refer to unit 5, step 3, to draw a diagonal line on the wrong side of each gold square. Using the gold squares and white rectangles, refer to unit 5 steps 8 and 9 and the chart below to make the number of pieced rectangles required for the quilt size you are making.

NUMBER OF PIECED RECTANGLES

2 x 3 Blocks	3 x 3 Blocks	3 x 4 Blocks
24	32	40

11. Arrange the pieced rectangles and the remaining white and red squares you cut in step 9 into rows. Sew the pieces in each row together and then sew the rows together.

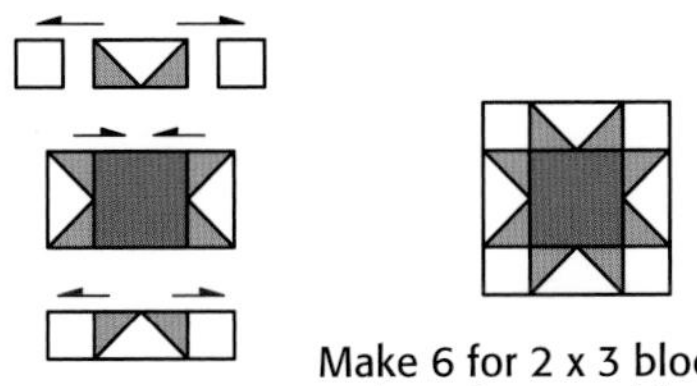

Make 6 for 2 x 3 block quilt.
Make 8 for 3 x 3 block quilt.
Make 10 for 3 x 4 block quilt.

ASSEMBLING THE QUILT TOP

1. Refer to the quilt diagram on page 56 to arrange the Stars Surrounded blocks, the pieced sashing strips, and the side and star sashing blocks into horizontal rows as shown. The placement of the sashing blocks for the 2 x 3 and 3 x 3 quilt plans will need to be changed slightly from the diagram shown so that the star sashing blocks are in each corner of the quilt top and the center of each sashing row; position the side sashing blocks along the outside edges of the quilt top with the white rectangles toward the outside. Stitch the pieces in each row together. Press the seams toward the sashing strips. Carefully pin the rows together to match seams. Sew the rows together. Press the seams toward the sashing rows.

2. Referring to "Straight-Cut Borders" (page 12), use the remaining red fabric to cut four 6"-wide strips the length of the fabric and sew them to the quilt.

FINISHING

Refer to "Backing and Batting" (page 13), "Layering and Basting" (page 14), "Quilting" (page 14), and "Binding" (page 14) as needed.

1. Piece the quilt backing as necessary. Center the quilt top and batting over the backing; baste.

2. Quilt as desired.

3. Trim the backing and batting. Cut the binding fabric into 2½"-wide bias strips. Sew the binding to the quilt.

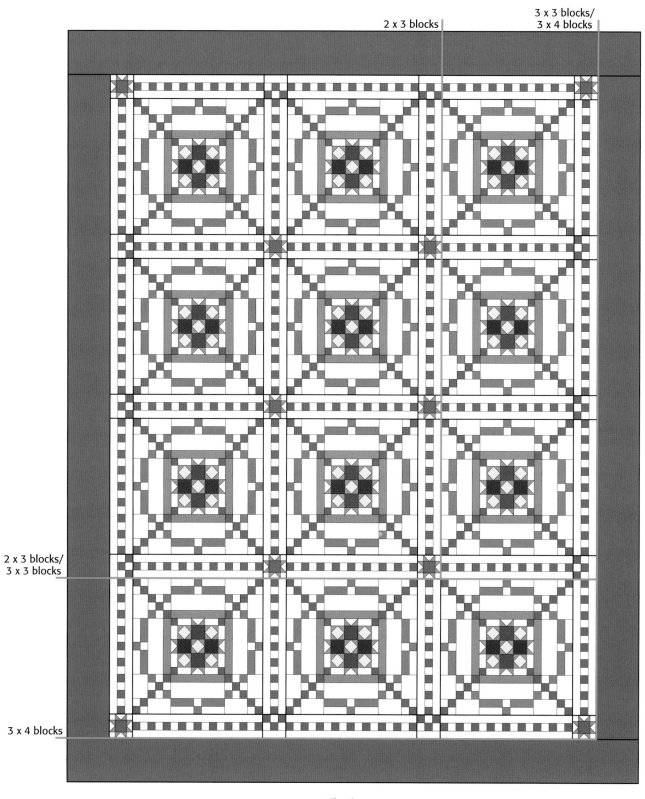

2 x 3 blocks

3 x 3 blocks/
3 x 4 blocks

2 x 3 blocks/
3 x 3 blocks

3 x 4 blocks

Quilt Diagram

DOUBLE BURGOYNE SURROUNDED

Making a Double Burgoyne Surrounded is double the fun. The diagonal line is stronger than in the Classic Burgoyne and gives the effect of a Double Irish Chain intersecting the blocks. The larger block makes it easy to use more colors and fabrics in your quilt and to make a quilt to fit a larger bed. Select a block size and refer to the corresponding columns in the charts as you work through the instructions. The quilt diagram on page 67 indicates setting plans for quilts of various sizes.

DOUBLE BURGOYNE SURROUNDED

By Elizabeth Hamby Carlson, 2003, Montgomery Village, Maryland, 95¾" x 95¾". Quilted by Leah Richard.

FINISHED BLOCK SIZES (Choose one.)

Block	Block Size
A	17"
B	21¼"

FINISHED QUILT SIZES

Block	2 x 3 Blocks	3 x 3 Blocks	3 x 4 Blocks
A	60" x 80"	80" x 80"	80" x 100"
B	70¾" x 95¾"	95¾" x 95¾"	95¾" x 120¾"

MATERIALS: 42"-WIDE FABRIC

Block A

Fabric	2 x 3 Blocks	3 x 3 Blocks	3 x 4 Blocks
White (block backgrounds, sashing)	2 yards	2⅝ yards	3⅜ yards
Pink #1 (blocks, sashing, middle border)	1⅜ yards	2 yards	2⅛ yards
Pink #2 (blocks)	¼ yard	¼ yard	⅜ yard
Pink #3 (blocks)	¼ yard	¼ yard	⅜ yard
Blue #1 (blocks, sashing, inner border, outer border, binding)	4⅝ yards	5 yards	6⅛ yards
Blue #2 (blocks)	¼ yard	¼ yard	⅜ yard
Blue #3 (blocks)	¼ yard	¼ yard	⅜ yard
Green #1 (blocks)	¼ yard	⅜ yard	⅜ yard
Green #2 (blocks)	¼ yard	⅜ yard	⅜ yard
Green #3 (blocks, sashing)	½ yard	½ yard	⅝ yard
Backing	5 yards	7⅜ yards	7⅜ yards
Batting	66" x 86"	86" x 86"	86" x 106"

Block B

Fabric	2 x 3 Blocks	3 x 3 Blocks	3 x 4 Blocks
White (block backgrounds, sashing)	3 yards	4 yards	4⅞ yards
Pink #1 (blocks, sashing, middle border)	2 yards	2⅜ yards	3 yards
Pink #2 (blocks)	¼ yard	¼ yard	⅜ yard
Pink #3 (blocks)	¼ yard	¼ yard	⅜ yard
Blue #1 (blocks, sashing, inner border, outer border, binding)	5⅞ yards	6½ yards	7⅞ yards
Blue #2 (blocks)	¼ yard	¼ yard	⅜ yard
Blue #3 (blocks)	¼ yard	¼ yard	⅜ yard
Green #1 (blocks)	⅜ yard	⅜ yard	½ yard
Green #2 (blocks)	⅜ yard	⅜ yard	½ yard
Green #3 (blocks, sashing)	½ yard	½ yard	¾ yard
Backing	5⅞ yards	8¾ yards	10¾ yards
Batting	77" x 102"	102" x 102"	102" x 127"

CUTTING STRIPS

Cut the required number of strips in the appropriate width to make the quilt size you have chosen. Cut all strips across the full width of the fabric, selvage to selvage. All measurements include ¼"-wide seam allowances. Refer to "Cutting Straight Strips" (page 8) for additional guidance as needed.

NUMBER AND WIDTH OF STRIPS

Block A

Fabric	Cut Width	2 × 3 Blocks	3 × 3 Blocks	3 × 4 Blocks
White	1½"	13	17	21
	2½"	7	10	13
	3½"	7	10	13
Pink #1	1½"	13	18	22
	3½"	2	4	4
Pink #2	3½"	1	1	2
Pink #3	3½"	1	1	2
Blue #1	1½"	19	26	33
	3½"	2	4	4
Blue #2	3½"	1	1	2
Blue #3	3½"	1	1	2
Green #1	3½"	1	2	2
Green #2	3½"	1	2	2
Green #3	1½"	5	5	6
	3½"	1*	1*	2*

COLOR OPTIONS: This quilt would have a contemporary look if made with bright primary colors and a very dark background. It would also be fun to make in a scrappier version, giving it a bit of the feel of the "Fat Quarter Fancy" quilt on page 38. To use a larger number of different fabrics, cut two shorter strip sets for each full-length set required. Gather fabrics and group them by value. Make sure you maintain enough value contrast between the background fabrics and the fabrics that define the pieced pattern.

Block B

Fabric	Cut Width	2 × 3 Blocks	3 × 3 Blocks	3 × 4 Blocks
White	1¾"	16	21	25
	3"	8	12	15
	4¼"	9	12	16
Pink #1	1¾"	14	20	27
	4¼"	4	4	6
Pink #2	4¼"	1	1	2
Pink #3	4¼"	1	1	2
Blue #1	1¾"	23	33	40
	4¼"	4	4	6
Blue #2	4¼"	1	1	2
Blue #3	4¼"	1	1	2
Green #1	4¼"	2	2	3
Green #2	4¼"	2	2	3
Green #3	1¾"	5	5	6
	4¼"	1*	1*	2*

Cut strip(s) in half crosswise.

MAKING THE BLOCK UNITS

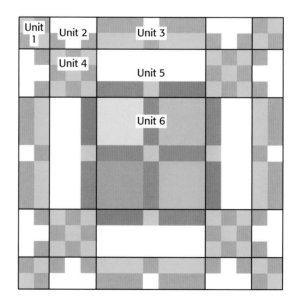

The Double Burgoyne Surrounded block is made up of six units. The units are the same in each block. Follow the step-by-step instructions to make each unit, referring to the chart to find the number of units required for the size quilt you have chosen. Note that the number of units required is the same for both block sizes.

UNIT REQUIREMENTS

Unit	2 x 3 Blocks	3 x 3 Blocks	3 x 4 Blocks
One	24	36	48
Two	48	72	96
Three	24	36	48
Four*	26	40	54
Five	24	36	48
Six	6	9	12

Some of these units will be set aside and used later for the center sashing blocks.

Unit 1

1. Make the required number of strip sets for the quilt size you have chosen, using one pink #1 strip and one blue #1 strip per set. For block A quilts, use 1½"-wide strips. For block B quilts, use 1¾"-wide strips. Refer to "Making Strip Sets" (page 10) as needed.

NUMBER OF STRIP SETS

Block	2 x 3 Blocks	3 x 3 Blocks	3 x 4 Blocks
A	2	3	4
B	3	4	5

2. Crosscut the strip sets into the required number of segments for the quilt size you are making. Cut the segments to the same width as the strip width used to make the strip sets (1½" or 1¾"). Refer to "Crosscutting Strip Sets" (page 10) for guidance. Note that the number of segments to cut is the same for both block sizes.

NUMBER OF SEGMENTS

2 x 3 Blocks	3 x 3 Blocks	3 x 4 Blocks
48	72	96

3. Stitch two segments together as shown to make unit 1.

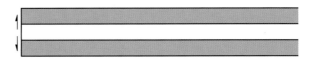

Unit 1

Unit 2

1. Make the required number of strip sets for the quilt size you have chosen, using two blue #1 strips and one white strip per set. For block A quilts, use 1½"-wide strips. For block B quilts, use 1¾"-wide strips.

NUMBER OF STRIP SETS

Block	2 x 3 Blocks	3 x 3 Blocks	3 x 4 Blocks
A	2	3	4
B	3	4	5

2. Crosscut the strip sets into segments the same width as the strip width used in the strip sets (1½" or 1¾"). Cut one segment for each unit 2 required.

3. Crosscut the white 1½"-wide strips (block A) or 1¾"-wide strips (block B) into rectangles. For block A quilts, cut the rectangles 1½" x 3½". For block B quilts, cut the rectangles 1¾" x 4¼". Cut one rectangle for each unit 2 required.

4. Stitch one segment and one rectangle together as shown to make unit 2.

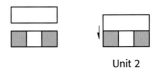

Unit 2

Unit 3

1. Make strip sets for rows 1 and 2 as shown, using two blue #1 or pink #1 wide strips and one white or blue #1 narrow strip per set. For block A quilts, use 1½"- and 3½"-wide strips. For block B quilts, use 1¾"- and 4¼"-wide strips. Note that the number of strip sets to make is the same for each row.

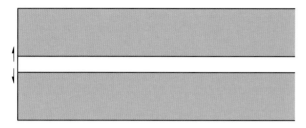

Row 1

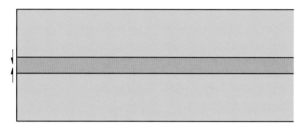

Row 2

NUMBER OF STRIP SETS
(Make this number for each row.)

Block	2 x 3 Blocks	3 x 3 Blocks	3 x 4 Blocks
A	1	2	2
B	2	2	3

2. Crosscut the strip sets into segments the same width as the narrow width used to make the strip sets (1½" or 1¾"). Cut one segment from both the row 1 and row 2 strip sets for each unit 3 required.

3. Sew one row 1 segment and one row 2 segment together as shown to make unit 3.

Unit 3

Unit 4

1. Make strip sets for rows 1 and 2 as shown, using the pink #1 and blue #1 strips. For block A quilts, use 1½"-wide strips. For block B quilts, use 1¾"-wide strips.

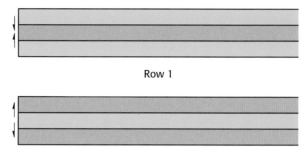

Row 1

Row 2

NUMBER OF STRIP SETS

Block	Row	2 x 3 Blocks	3 x 3 Blocks	3 x 4 Blocks
A	1	3	4	5
	2	2	3	3
B	1	3	5	6
	2	2	3	4

2. Crosscut the strip sets into segments the same width as the strip width used to make the strip sets (1½" or 1¾"). Note that the number to cut is the same for both block sizes.

NUMBER OF SEGMENTS*

Row	2 x 3 Blocks	3 x 3 Blocks	3 x 4 Blocks
1	58	88	118
2	36	52	68

Some of these segments will be set aside and used later for the sashing blocks.

3. Sew two row 1 segments and one row 2 segment together as shown to make unit 4, referring to the unit requirements chart on page 61 for the number to make. Set aside the remaining segments for the side and corner sashing blocks.

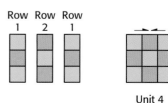

Row 1   Row 2   Row 1

Unit 4

Unit 5

1. Make the required number of strip sets as shown, using one wide strip *each* of green #1 and green #2 and one narrow strip of pink #1. For block A quilts, use 1½"- and 3½"-wide strips. For block B quilts, use 1¾"- and 4¼"-wide strips.

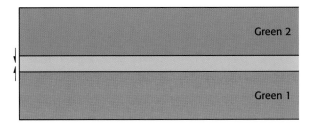

NUMBER OF STRIP SETS

Block	2 x 3 Blocks	3 x 3 Blocks	3 x 4 Blocks
A	1	2	2
B	2	2	3

2. Crosscut the strip sets into segments the same width as the pink #1 strip (1½" or 1¾"). Cut one segment for each unit 5 required.

3. Crosscut the white 2½"-wide strips (block A) or 3"-wide strips (block B) into rectangles. For block A quilts, cut the rectangles 2½" x 7½". For block B quilts, cut the rectangles 3" x 9¼". Cut one rectangle for each unit 5 required.

4. Stitch one segment and one rectangle together as shown to make unit 5.

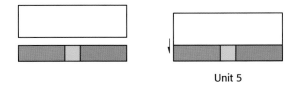

Unit 5

Unit 6

1. Crosscut 3½"-wide strips (block A) or 4¼"-wide strips (block B) of pink #2, pink #3, blue #2, and blue #3 into squares the same size as the strip width. Cut one square of *each* fabric for each unit 6 required. Crosscut the 1½"-wide strips (block A) or 1¾"-wide strips (block B) of green #3 into rectangles. For block A quilts, cut the rectangles 1½" x 3½". For block B quilts, cut the rectangles 1¾" x 4¼". Cut two rectangles for each unit 6 required.

2. Stitch the squares and rectangles into rows 1 and 3 as shown.

Row 1   Row 3

3. Make the required number of row 2 strip sets as shown, using the half-length 3½"-wide (block A) or 4¼"-wide (block B) green #3 strips and 1½"-wide (block A) or 1¾"-wide (block B) pink #1 strips.

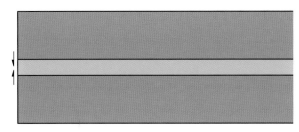

Row 2

NUMBER OF STRIP SETS

Block	2 x 3 Blocks	3 x 3 Blocks	3 x 4 Blocks
A	1	1	2
B	1	1	2

4. Crosscut the strip sets into segments the same width as the pink #1 strips (1½" or 1¾"). Cut one segment for each unit 6 required.

5. Stitch one each of rows 1, 2, and 3 together as shown to make unit 6.

Note: In the quilt shown on page 58, the row 1 and row 3 units were rotated in every other block to add variety to the quilt.

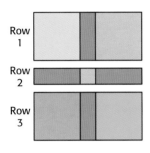

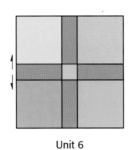

Unit 6

Assembling the Blocks

Arrange the units into rows as shown. Stitch the units in each row together. Press the seams in the directions indicated. Sew the rows together. Press the seams in the directions indicated. Set aside the remaining unit 4 units for the center sashing blocks.

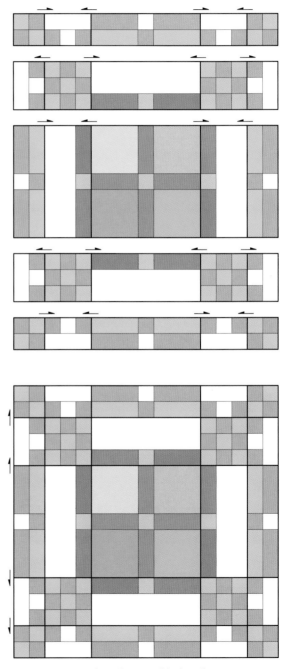

Make 6 for 2 x 3 block quilt.
Make 9 for 3 x 3 block quilt.
Make 12 for 3 x 4 block quilt.

Making the Sashing

1. Make strip sets for the end and center segments of the pieced sashing strips used in the center of the quilt top as shown, using 1½"-wide strips (block A) or 1¾"-wide strips (block B) of blue #1, green #3, and white.

End

Center

NUMBER OF STRIP SETS

Block	Strip Set	2 x 3 Blocks	3 x 3 Blocks	3 x 4 Blocks
A	End	1	1	2
	Center	1	1	1
B	End	1	2	2
	Center	1	1	1

2. Crosscut the strip sets into segments the same width as the strip width used to make the strip sets (1½" or 1¾"). Note that the number of segments to cut is the same for both block sizes.

NUMBER OF SEGMENTS

Strip Set	2 x 3 Blocks	3 x 3 Blocks	3 x 4 Blocks
End	14	24	34
Center	7	12	17

3. Make strip sets for the end and center segments of the pieced sashing strips used on the sides of the quilt top as shown, using 1½"-wide strips (block A) or 1¾"-wide strips (block B) of blue #1 and green #3, and white 2½"-wide strips (block A) or 3"-wide strips (block B).

End

Center

NUMBER OF STRIP SETS

Block	Strip Set	2 x 3 Blocks	3 x 3 Blocks	3 x 4 Blocks
A	End	1	1	2
	Center	1	1	1
B	End	1	2	2
	Center	1	1	1

4. Crosscut the strip sets into segments the same width as the narrow strip width used to make the strip sets (1½" or 1¾"). Note that the number of segments to cut is the same for both block sizes.

NUMBER OF SEGMENTS

Strip Set	2 x 3 Blocks	3 x 3 Blocks	3 x 4 Blocks
End	20	24	28
Center	10	12	14

5. Crosscut the white 3½"-wide strips (block A) or 4¼"-wide strips (block B) into the number of sashing rectangles required for the quilt size you are making. For block A quilts, cut the rectangles 3½" x 7½". For block B quilts, cut the rectangles 4¼" x 9¼". Note that the number to cut is the same for both block sizes.

NUMBER OF SASHING RECTANGLES

2 x 3 Blocks	3 x 3 Blocks	3 x 4 Blocks
34	48	62

6. Using two of the appropriate end segments, one of the appropriate center segments, and two rectangles, make the number of center and side sashing strips required for the quilt size you are making as shown.

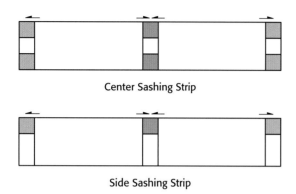

Center Sashing Strip

Side Sashing Strip

NUMBER OF SASHING STRIPS

Sashing	2 x 3 Blocks	3 x 3 Blocks	3 x 4 Blocks
Center	7	12	17
Side	10	12	14

7. To make the side and corner sashing blocks, make one *each* of the row 3 and row 4 strip sets as shown, using 1½"-wide strips (block A) or 1¾"-wide strips (block B) of white, blue #1, and pink #1.

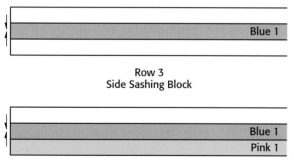

Blue 1

Row 3
Side Sashing Block

Blue 1
Pink 1

Row 4
Corner Sashing Block

8. Crosscut the strip sets into segments the same width as the strip width used to make the strip sets (1½" or 1¾").

NUMBER OF SEGMENTS

Row	2 x 3 Blocks	3 x 3 Blocks	3 x 4 Blocks
3	6	8	10
4	8	8	8

9. Arrange the row 1 and 2 segments set aside from unit 4 and the row 3 and 4 segments into rows as shown. Stitch the rows together.

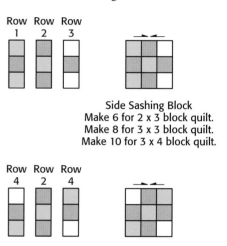

Row 1 Row 2 Row 3

Side Sashing Block
Make 6 for 2 x 3 block quilt.
Make 8 for 3 x 3 block quilt.
Make 10 for 3 x 4 block quilt.

Row 4 Row 2 Row 4

Corner Sashing Block
Make 4 for all quilt sizes.

ASSEMBLING THE QUILT TOP

1. Refer to the quilt diagram to arrange the Double Burgoyne Surrounded blocks, the center and side sashing strips, and the side, center, and corner sashing blocks into horizontal rows as shown. The placement of the sashing blocks for the 2 x 3 and 3 x 3 quilt plans will need to be changed slightly from the diagram shown so that the corner sashing blocks are in each corner and the side sashing blocks are positioned along the outside of the quilt top with the row 3 segments toward the outside of the quilt. Stitch the pieces in each row together. Press the seams toward the sashing strips. Carefully pin the rows together to match seams. Sew the rows together. Press the seams toward the sashing rows.

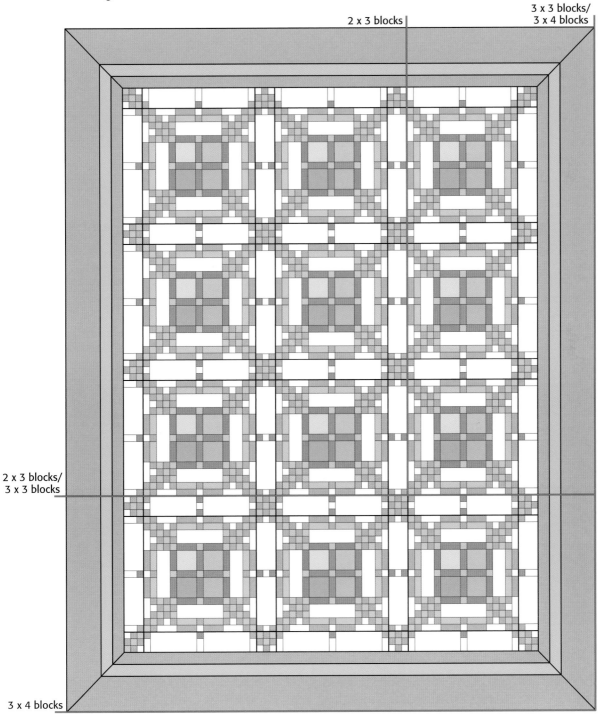

Quilt Diagram

2. Refer to "Mitered Borders" (page 12) as needed to cut four 2¼"-wide inner border strips and four 5¾"-wide outer border strips to the length needed along the length of the remaining blue #1 fabric. For the middle border, cut the number of 2"-wide strips required for the quilt size you are making across the width of the remaining pink #1 fabric.

NUMBER OF MIDDLE BORDER STRIPS

Block	2 x 3 Blocks	3 x 3 Blocks	3 x 4 Blocks
A	7	8	9
B	9	10	11

3. Sew the middle border strips together end to end to make one continuous strip. From this strip, cut two side middle border strips equal to the full, finished length of the quilt plus 1", and two top and bottom middle border strips equal to the full finished width of the quilt plus 1".

4. Sew the inner, middle, and outer border strips together to make two side border units and two top and bottom border units. Press the seams toward the middle border.

5. Refer to "Mitered Borders" (page 12) as needed to add the border units to the sides, top, and bottom of the quilt. Miter the corners; press.

FINISHING

Refer to "Backing and Batting" (page 13), "Layering and Basting" (page 14), "Quilting" (page 14), and "Binding" (page 14) as needed.

1. Piece the quilt backing as necessary. Center the quilt top and batting over the backing; baste.

2. Quilt as desired.

3. Trim the backing and batting. Cut the binding fabric into 2½"-wide bias strips. Sew the binding to the quilt.

BURGOYNE'S PINWHEELS

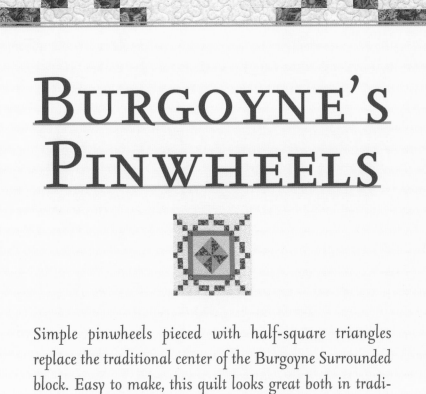

Simple pinwheels pieced with half-square triangles replace the traditional center of the Burgoyne Surrounded block. Easy to make, this quilt looks great both in traditional colors and in bright, contemporary fabrics. Select a block size and follow the appropriate color-coded charts. The quilt diagram on page 78 shows setting plans for quilts of various sizes.

BURGOYNE'S PINWHEELS

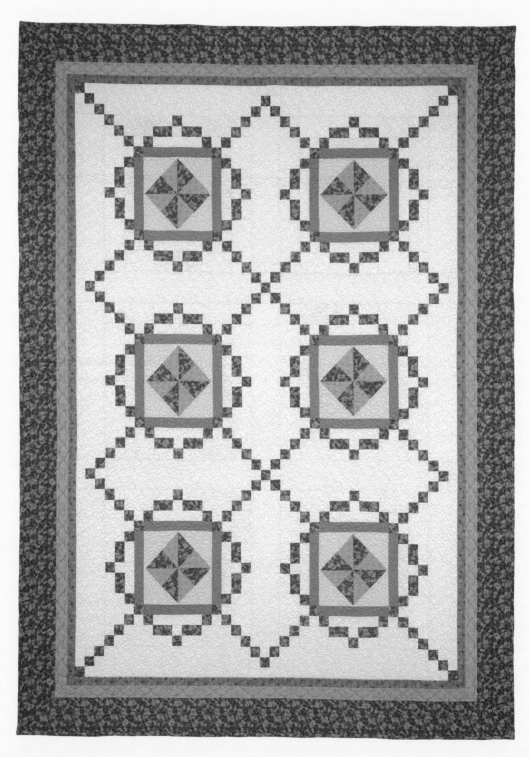

By Elizabeth Hamby Carlson, 2003, Montgomery Village, Maryland, 62¼" x 84¾". Quilted by Leah Richard.

FINISHED BLOCK SIZES (Choose one.)

Block	Block Size
A	15"
B	18¾"

FINISHED QUILT SIZES

Block	2 x 3 Blocks	3 x 3 Blocks	3 x 4 Blocks
A	52" x 70"	70" x 70"	70" x 88"
B	61¾" x 84¼"	84¼" x 84¼"	84¼" x 106¾"

MATERIALS: 42"-WIDE FABRIC

Block A

Fabric	2 x 3 Blocks	3 x 3 Blocks	3 x 4 Blocks
Ivory (block backgrounds)	2⅜ yards	3¼ yards	3⅞ yards
Brown floral (blocks, outer border, binding)	3¼ yards	3⅝ yards	4¾ yards
Medium green (blocks)	⅜ yard	½ yard	½ yard
Tan (blocks)	⅜ yard	½ yard	½ yard
Pink #1 (blocks)	⅜ yard	⅜ yard	½ yard
Green (inner border)	½ yard	½ yard	½ yard
Pink #2 (middle border)	½ yard	⅝ yard	⅝ yard
Backing	4½ yards	4½ yards	5⅜ yards
Batting	58" x 78"	78" x 78"	78" x 94"

Block B

Fabric	2 x 3 Blocks	3 x 3 Blocks	3 x 4 Blocks
Ivory (block backgrounds)	3¼ yards	3⅞ yards	5¼ yards
Brown floral (blocks, outer border, binding)	4⅛ yards	4¼ yards	5¾ yards
Medium green (blocks)	½ yard	⅝ yard	¾ yard
Tan (blocks)	½ yard	⅝ yard	¾ yard
Pink #1 (blocks)	⅜ yard	⅜ yard	½ yard
Green (inner border)	½ yard	½ yard	⅝ yard
Pink #2 (middle border)	⅝ yard	⅝ yard	¾ yard
Backing	5¼ yards	7¾ yards	9½ yards
Batting	68" x 91"	91" x 91"	91" x 113"

Cutting Strips

Cut the required number of strips in the appropriate width to make the quilt size you have chosen. Cut all strips across the full width of the fabric, selvage to selvage. All measurements include ¼"-wide seam allowances. Refer to "Cutting Straight Strips" (page 8) for additional guidance as needed.

NUMBER AND WIDTH OF STRIPS

Block A

Fabric	Cut Width	2 x 3 Blocks	3 x 3 Blocks	3 x 4 Blocks
Ivory	1½"	9	12	14
	2½"	9	13	15
	3½"	9	12	16
	5½"	1	2	2
Brown	1½"	11	16	18
	2½"	2	4	4
	3⅜"	2	2	3
Medium green	1½"	5	8	10
Tan	4½"	2	3	3
Pink #1	3⅜"	2	2	3

Block B

Fabric	Cut Width	2 x 3 Blocks	3 x 3 Blocks	3 x 4 Blocks
Ivory	1¾"	11	13	17
	3"	11	13	18
	4¼"	9	12	16
	6¾"	2	2	3
Brown	1¾"	15	17	22
	3"	4	4	6
	3⅞"	2	2	3
Medium green	1¾"	6	9	12
Tan	5½"	2	3	4
Pink #1	3⅞"	2	2	3

Making the Block Units

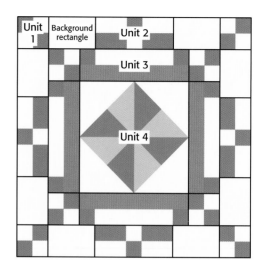

The Burgoyne's Pinwheel block is made up of four units and one background rectangle. The units and rectangles are the same in each block. Follow the step-by-step instructions to make each unit, referring to the chart to find the number of units required for the size quilt you have chosen. Note that the number of units required is the same for both block sizes. The cutting instructions for the background rectangle will be given later.

UNIT REQUIREMENTS

Unit	2 x 3 Blocks	3 x 3 Blocks	3 x 4 Blocks
One	48	72	96
Two	24	36	48
Three	24	36	48
Four	6	9	12

Unit 1

1. Make the required number of strip sets using one ivory and one brown strip per set as shown. For block A quilts, use 1½"-wide strips. For block B quilts, use 1¾"-wide strips. Refer to "Making Strip Sets" (page 10) as needed.

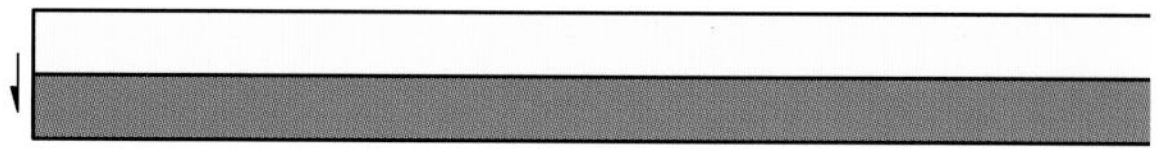

NUMBER OF STRIP SETS

Block	2 x 3 Blocks	3 x 3 Blocks	3 x 4 Blocks
A	4	6	8
B	5	7	9

2. Crosscut the strip sets into segments the same width as the strip width used to make the strip sets (1½" or 1¾"). Refer to "Crosscutting Strip Sets" (page 10) for guidance. Note that the number of segments to cut is the same for both block sizes.

NUMBER OF SEGMENTS

2 x 3 Blocks	3 x 3 Blocks	3 x 4 Blocks
96	144	192

3. Stitch two segments together as shown to make unit 1.

Unit 1

Unit Two

1. Make strip sets for rows 1 and 2 as shown, using two wide brown or ivory strips and one narrow brown or ivory strip per set. For block A quilts, use 1½"- and 2½"-wide strips. For block B quilts, use 1¾"- and 3"-wide strips. Note that the number to cut is the same for both rows.

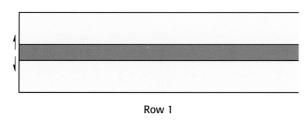

Row 1

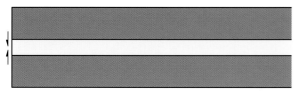

Row 2

NUMBER OF STRIP SETS

Block	2 x 3 Blocks	3 x 3 Blocks	3 x 4 Blocks
A	1	2	2
B	2	2	3

2. Crosscut the strip sets into segments the same width as the strip width used to make the strip sets (1½" or 1¾"). Cut one segment from the row 1 and row 2 strip sets for each unit 2 required.

3. Sew one row 1 segment and one row 2 segment together as shown to make unit 2.

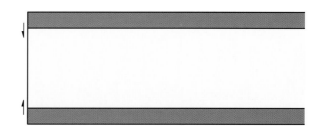

Unit 2

Unit 3

1. Make the strip set(s) as shown, using two narrow brown strips and one wide ivory strip. For block A quilts, use 1½"- and 5½"-wide strips. For block B quilts, use 1¾"- and 6¾"-wide strips.

NUMBER OF STRIP SETS

Block	2 x 3 Blocks	3 x 3 Blocks	3 x 4 Blocks
A	1	2	2
B	2	2	3

2. Crosscut the strip sets into segments the same width as the narrow strip width used to make the strip sets (1½" or 1¾"). Cut one segment for each unit 3 required.

3. Crosscut the medium green 1½"-wide strips (block A) or 1¾"-wide strips (block B) into rectangles. For block A quilts, cut the rectangles 1½" x 7½". For block B quilts, cut the rectangles 1¾" x 9¼". Cut one rectangle for each unit 3 required.

4. Stitch one segment and one rectangle together as shown to make unit 3.

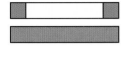 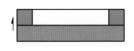

Unit 3

Unit 4

1. Layer one 3⅜"-wide strip (block A) or 3⅞"-wide strip (block B) *each* of pink #1 and brown, right sides together. Crosscut the paired strips into squares the same size as the strip width. Note that the number to cut is the same for both block sizes. Cut each pair of squares in half once diagonally to yield two sets of layered triangles. Do not separate the triangles.

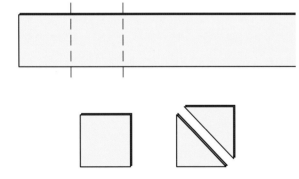

NUMBER OF SQUARES

2 x 3 Blocks	3 x 3 Blocks	3 x 4 Blocks
12	18	24

2. Sew each layered pair of triangles together along the long edge to make half-square-triangle units. Press the seams toward the brown triangles.

3. Stitch four half-square triangle units together as shown to make a pinwheel unit.

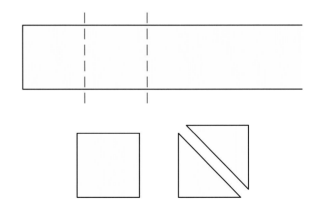

4. Crosscut the tan 4½"-wide strips (block A) or 5½"-wide strips (block B) into squares the same size as the strip width. Note that the number to cut is the same for both block sizes. Cut each square in half once diagonally to yield two triangles.

NUMBER OF SQUARES

2 x 3 Blocks	3 x 3 Blocks	3 x 4 Blocks
12	18	24

5. Sew a tan triangle to opposite sides of each pin-wheel unit. Press seams toward the tan triangles. Repeat for the remaining sides of the pinwheel units. The resulting squares will be somewhat oversized unit 4s. Square up the units so that each one measures 7½" (block A) or 9¼" (block B).

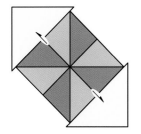 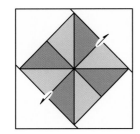

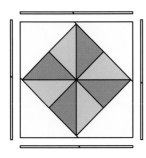

CUTTING THE BACKGROUND RECTANGLES

Crosscut the ivory 2½"-wide strips (block A) or 3"-wide strips (block B) into the background rectangles. For block A quilts, cut the rectangles 2½" x 3½". For block B quilts, cut the rectangles 3" x 4¼". Note that the number to cut is the same for both block sizes.

NUMBER OF RECTANGLES

2 x 3 Blocks	3 x 3 Blocks	3 x 4 Blocks
48	72	96

ASSEMBLING THE BLOCKS

1. Stitch a unit 3 to the sides of each unit 4 as shown. Stitch a unit 1 to each end of the remaining unit 3s, then stitch these pieced strips to the top and bottom of each unit 4 as shown.

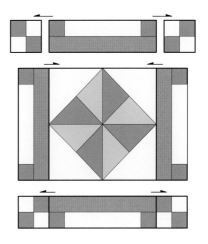

Detail of the center of an assembled block.

2. Sew a background rectangle to the ends of each unit 2 as shown. Stitch the pieced strips to the sides of the units from step 1. Stitch a unit 1 to the ends of the remaining pieced strips as shown. Stitch these strips to the top and bottom of the pieced units to complete the blocks.

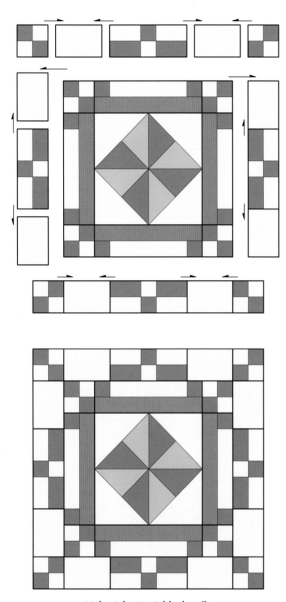

Make 6 for 2 x 3 block quilt.
Make 9 for 3 x 3 block quilt.
Make 12 for 3 x 4 block quilt.

MAKING THE SASHING

1. Crosscut the required number of strips from the 3½"-wide (block A) or 4¼"-wide (block B) ivory strips. For block A quilts, cut 3½" x 15½" strips. For block B quilts, cut 4¼" x 19¼" strips. Note that the number of sashing strips is the same for both block sizes.

NUMBER OF SASHING STRIPS

2 x 3 Blocks	3 x 3 Blocks	3 x 4 Blocks
17	24	31

2. Make one strip set *each* for rows 1, 2, and 3 of the center, side, and corner sashing blocks as shown, using the brown and ivory strips. For block A quilts, use 1½"-wide brown strips and 1½"- and 2½"-wide ivory strips. For block B quilts, use 1¾"-wide brown strips and 1¾"- and 3"-wide ivory strips.

Row 1

Row 2

Row 3

3. Crosscut the strip sets into segments the same width as the narrow strip width used to make the strip sets (1½" or 1¾"). Note that the number of segments to cut is the same for both block sizes.

NUMBER OF SEGMENTS

Row	2 x 3 Blocks	3 x 3 Blocks	3 x 4 Blocks
1	10	16	22
2	12	16	20
3	8	8	8

4. Crosscut the ivory 1½"-wide strips (block A) or 1¾"-wide strips (block B) into rectangles for the side sashing blocks. For block A quilts, cut 1½" x 3½" rectangles. For block B quilts, cut 1¾" x 4¼" rectangles. Note that the number to cut is the same for both block sizes.

NUMBER OF RECTANGLES

2 x 3 Blocks	3 x 3 Blocks	3 x 4 Blocks
6	8	10

5. For each block, arrange the segments and rectangles into rows as shown. Stitch the rows together.

Center Sashing Block
Make 2 for 2 x 3 block quilt.
Make 4 for 3 x 3 block quilt.
Make 6 for 3 x 4 block quilt.

Side Sashing Block
Make 6 for 2 x 3 block quilt.
Make 8 for 3 x 3 block quilt.
Make 10 for 3 x 4 block quilt.

Corner Sashing Block
Make 4 for all quilt sizes.

ASSEMBLING THE QUILT TOP

1. Refer to the quilt diagram on page 78 to arrange the Burgoyne's Pinwheel blocks, the sashing rectangles, and the sashing blocks into horizontal rows. The placement of the sashing blocks for the 2 x 3 and 3 x 3 quilt plans will need to be changed slightly from the diagram shown so that the corner sashing blocks are in each corner and the side sashing blocks are positioned on the outside edges with the ivory rectangles toward the outside of the quilt. Stitch the pieces in each row together. Press the seams toward the sashing rectangles. Carefully pin the rows together to match seams. Sew the rows together. Press the seams toward the sashing rows.

2. Cut the green inner border fabric into the required number of 1½"-wide strips for the quilt size you are making. Cut the same number of 2"-wide strips from the pink #2 middle border fabric.

NUMBER OF INNER AND MIDDLE BORDER STRIPS

Block	2 x 3 Blocks	3 x 3 Blocks	3 x 4 Blocks
A	7	8	8
B	8	9	10

3. Sew the inner border strips together end to end to make one continuous strip. From this strip cut two side inner border strips equal to the full, finished length of the quilt plus 1", and two top and bottom inner border strips equal to the full finished width of the quilt plus 1". Repeat with the middle border strips.

4. From the brown fabric, cut 4½"-wide strips along the length of the fabric. Cut two side outer border strips equal to the full, finished length of the quilt plus 1", and two top and bottom outer border strips equal to the full finished width of the quilt plus 1".

5. Refer to "Mitered Borders" (page 12) as needed to sew the inner, middle, and outer border strips together to make two side border units and two top and bottom border units. Press the seams toward the middle border strips. Stitch the units to the sides, top, and bottom of the quilt. Miter the corners; press.

FINISHING

Refer to "Backing and Batting" (page 13), "Layering and Basting" (page 14), "Quilting" (page 14), and "Binding" (page 14) as needed.

1. Piece the quilt backing as necessary. Center the quilt top and batting over the backing; baste.

2. Quilt as desired.

3. Trim the backing and batting. Cut the binding fabric into 2½"-wide bias strips. Sew the binding to the quilt.

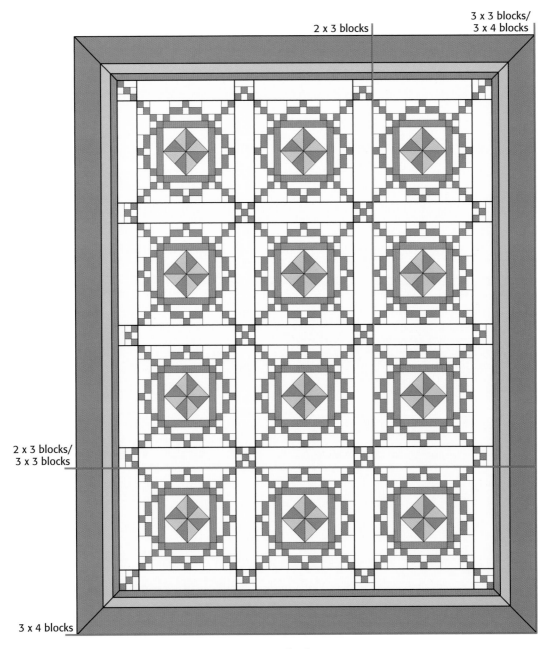

Quilt Diagram

BIBLIOGRAPHY

Better Homes & Gardens Books. *America's Heritage Quilts*. Des Moines, Iowa: Meredith Corporation, 1991.

Carlson, Elizabeth Hamby. *Small Wonders: Tiny Treasures in Patchwork and Appliqué*. Woodinville, Washington: Martingale & Company, 1999.

————. *Trip to Ireland: Quilts Combining Two Old Favorites*. Woodinville, Washington: Martingale & Company, 2002.

Dietrich, Mimi. *Hand Appliqué*. Woodinville, Washington: Martingale & Company, 1998.

————. *Happy Endings: Finishing the Edges of Your Quilt*. Woodinville, Washington: That Patchwork Place, 1987.

Kiracofe, Roderick. *The American Quilt: A History of Cloth and Comfort 1750–1950*. New York, New York: Clarkson Potter, 1993.

Martin, Nancy. *Threads of Time*. Woodinville, Washington: That Patchwork Place, 1990.

ABOUT THE AUTHOR

SINCE MAKING HER first quilt in 1978, Elizabeth Hamby Carlson has made more quilts than she can count and always has at least a dozen more in the planning stages. She began teaching quiltmaking in 1983 and especially enjoys sharing her methods for hand appliqué, machine piecing, and miniature quiltmaking. Through her pattern business, Elizabeth Quilts, she markets original quilt patterns reflecting her interest in the decorative arts and quilting traditions of the eighteenth and nineteenth centuries. In addition to her traditional quilts, Elizabeth, a lifelong Anglophile, also designs and makes quilts inspired by her interest in English history. Her award-winning quilts have been featured in numerous quilt publications, and she has appeared on HGTV's *Simply Quilts*. *Burgoyne Surrounded* is her third book for Martingale & Company.

Raised in northeastern Ohio, Elizabeth lives with her husband in Montgomery Village, Maryland. She has a grown son and daughter, each of whom has lots of quilts. When Elizabeth is not quilting, she enjoys reading, antiquing, and planning her next trip to England.